INSPIRING QUOTES ABOUT DOING YOUR BEST

A Motivational Coloring Book to Fuel Your Success

Russell Sylvester Byrne

MORE BOOKS FROM THE AUTHOR

scan this with your camera

THIS BOOK BELONGS TO

TO

....

....

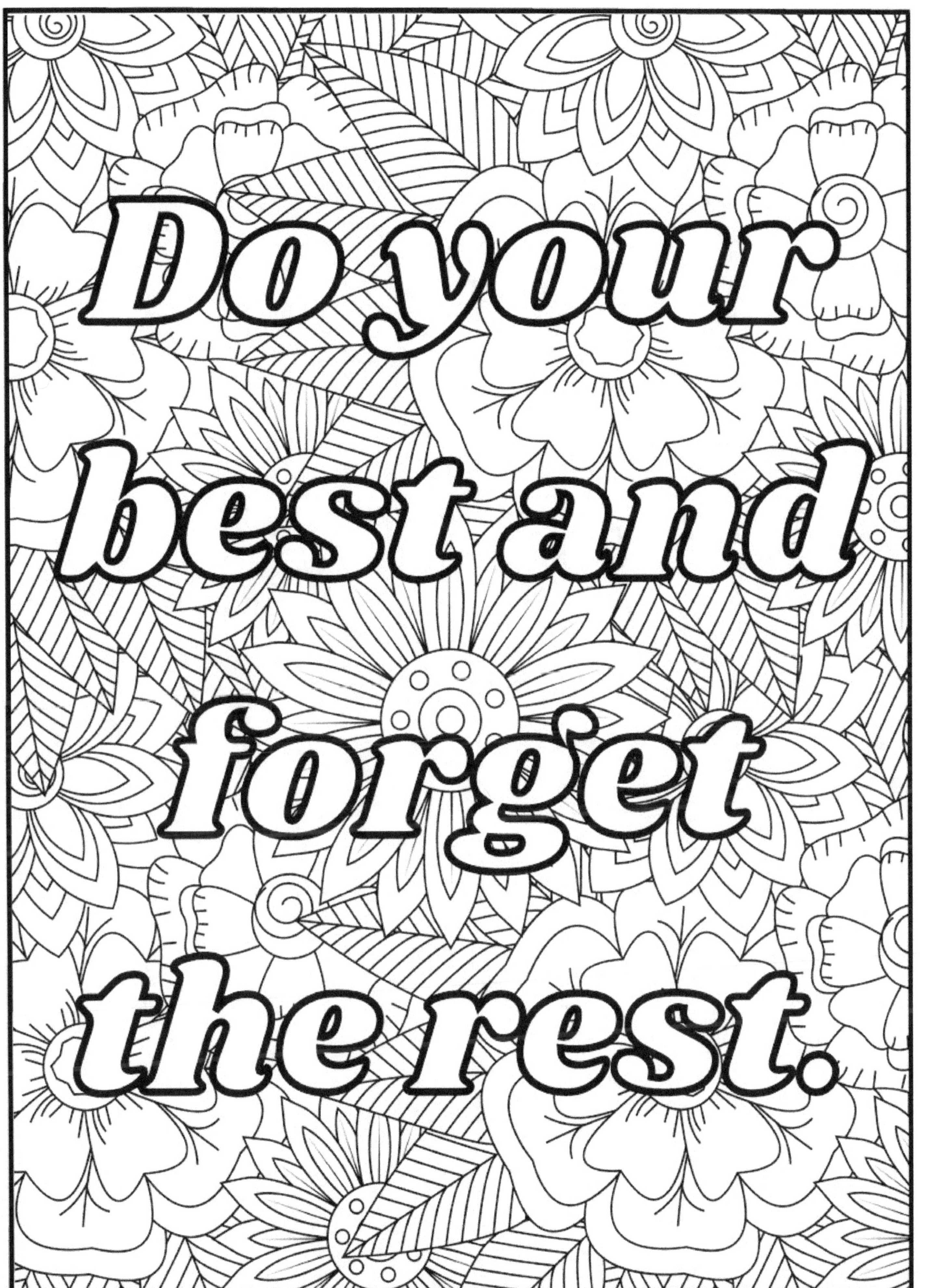

Do your best and forget the rest.

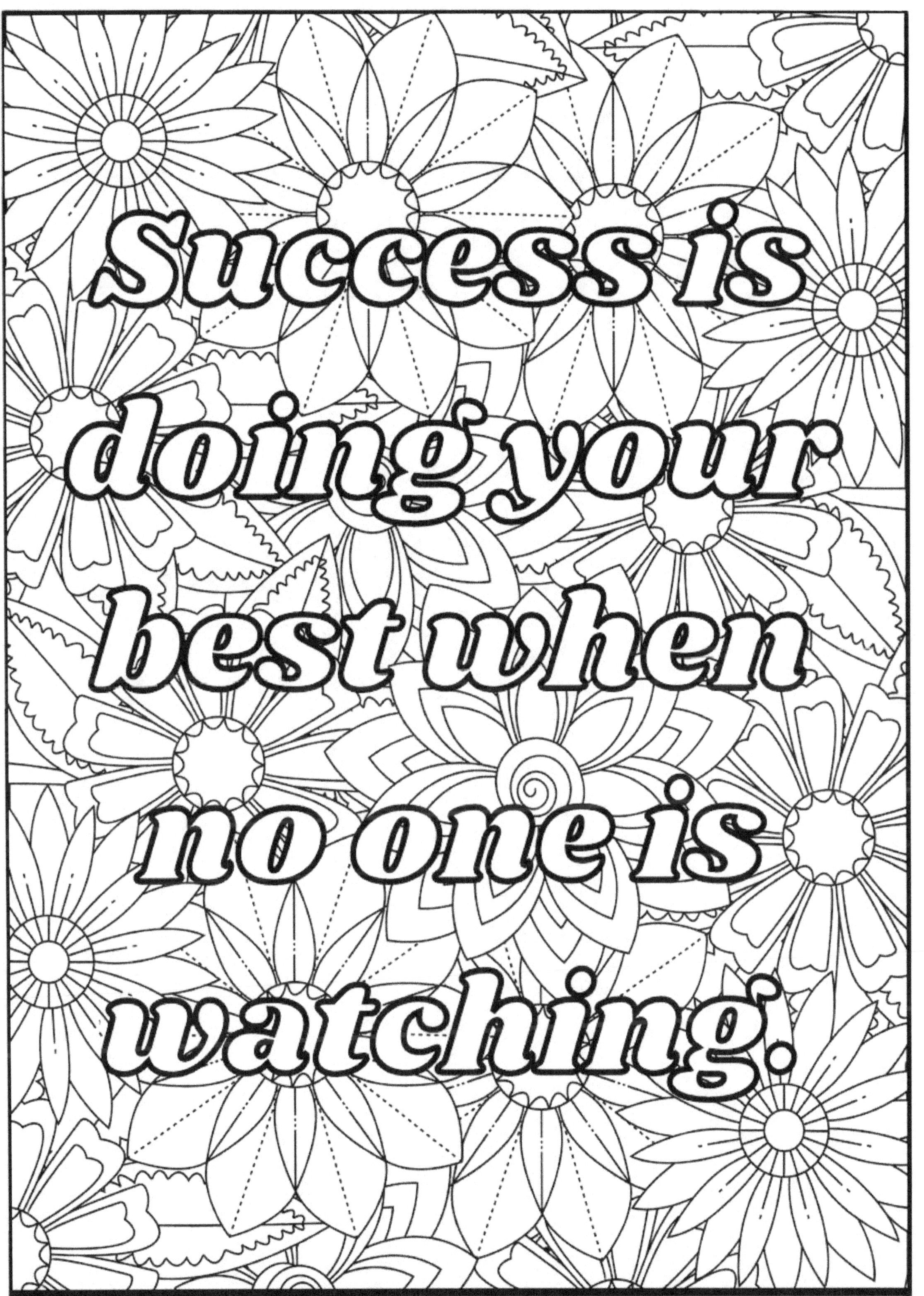

Success is doing your best when no one is watching.

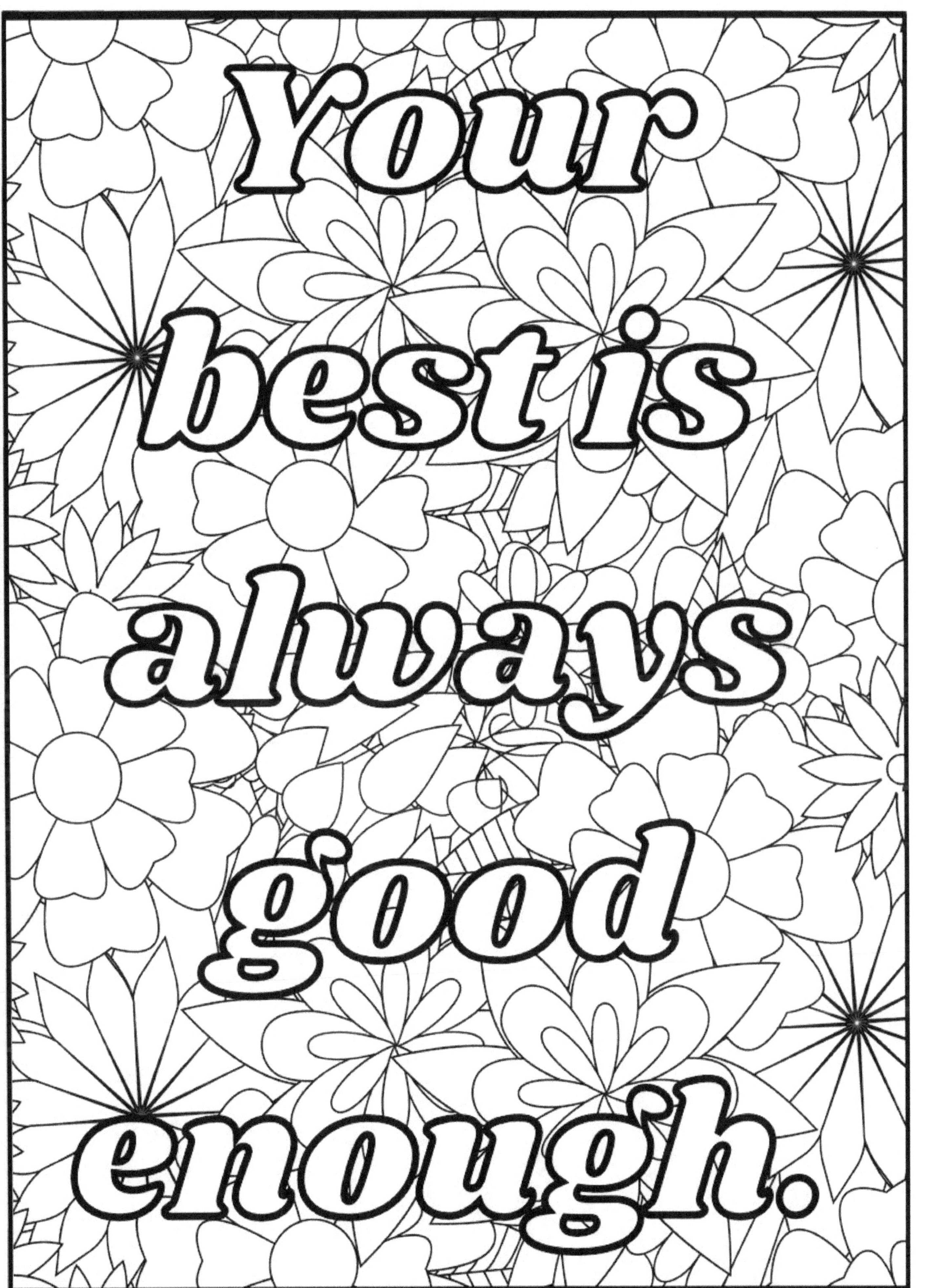
Your
best is
always
good
enough.

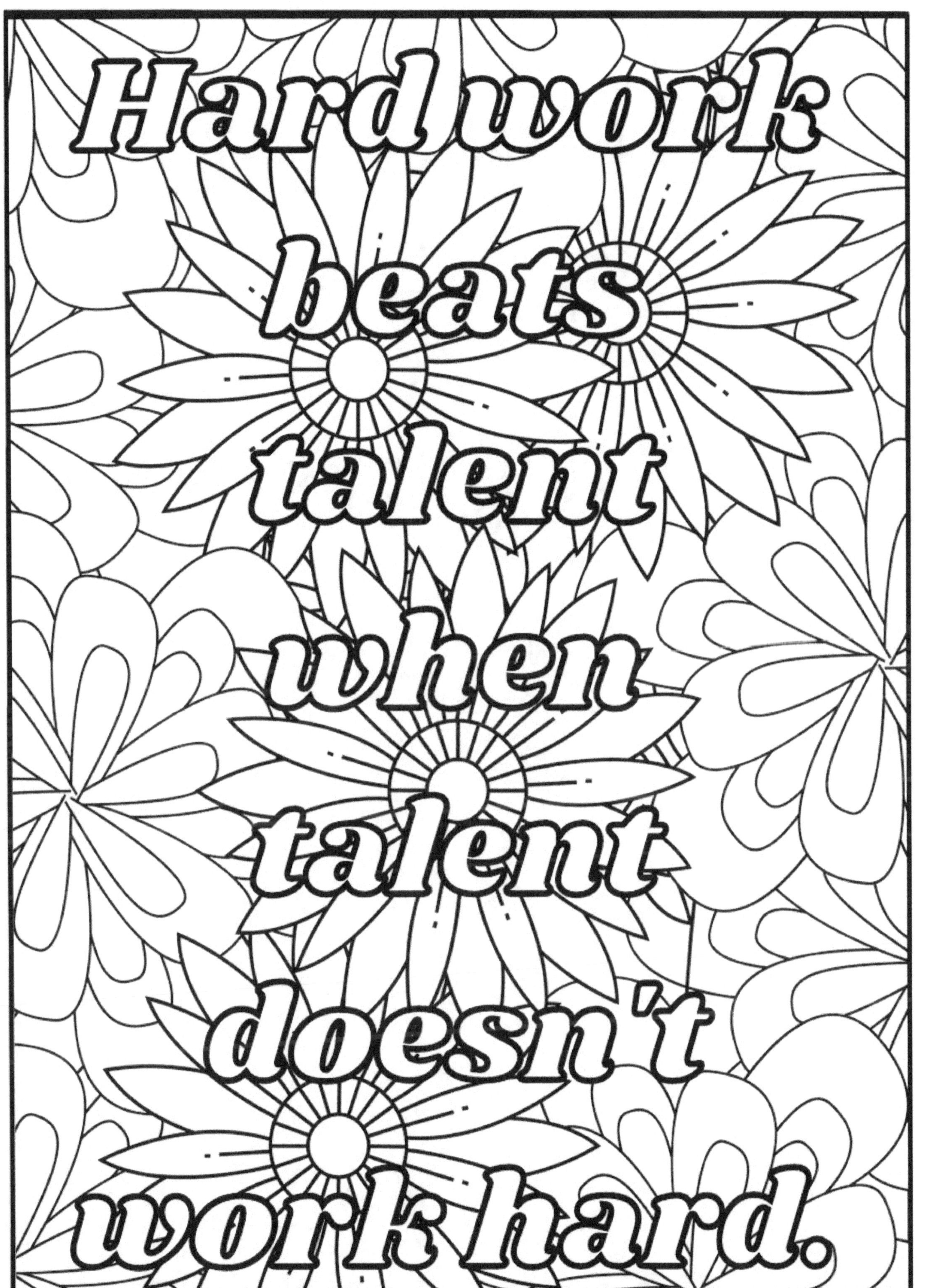

Hard work
beats
talent
when
talent
doesn't
work hard.

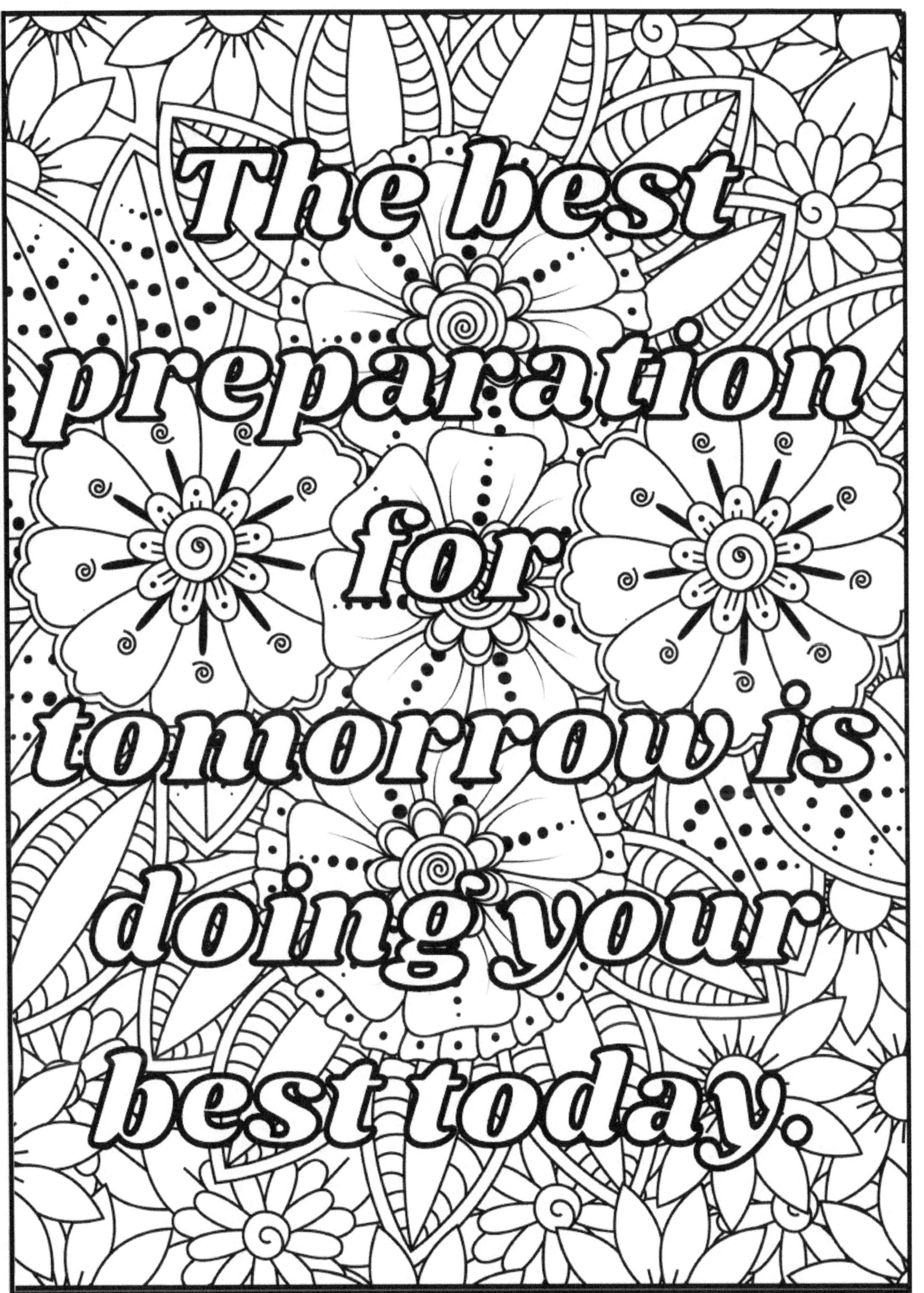
The best preparation for tomorrow is doing your best today.

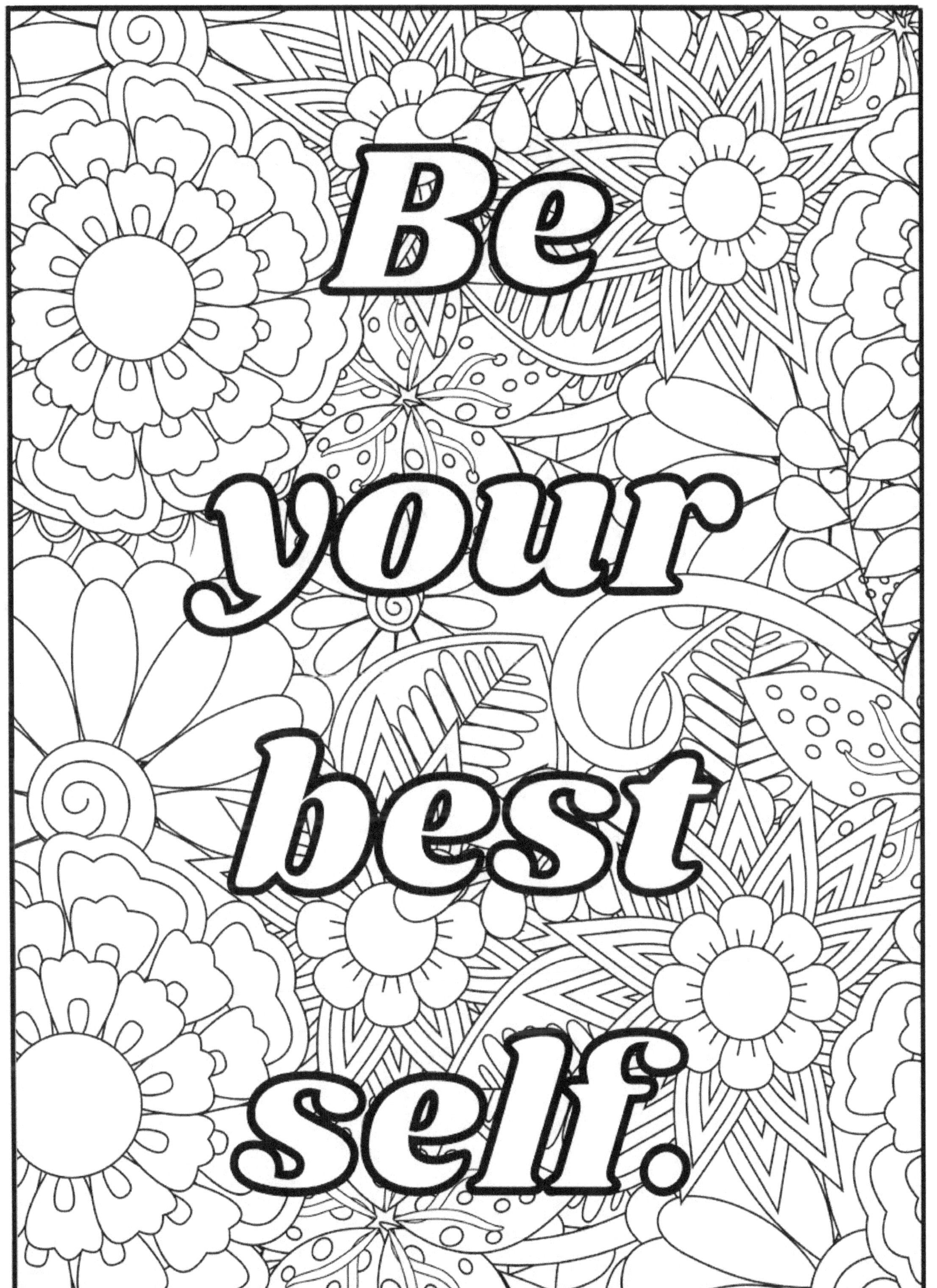

Be
your
best
self.

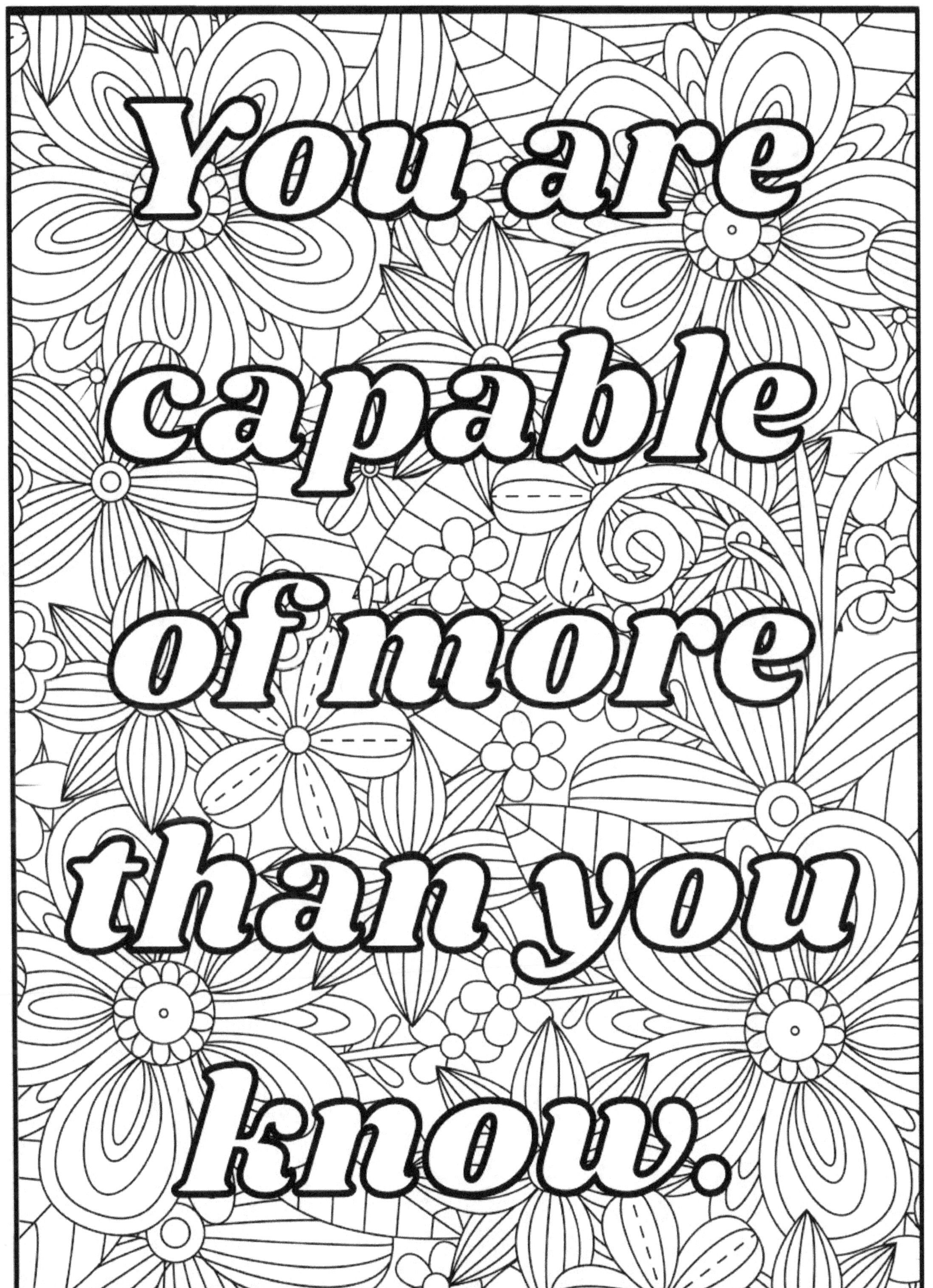

You are
capable
of more
than you
know.

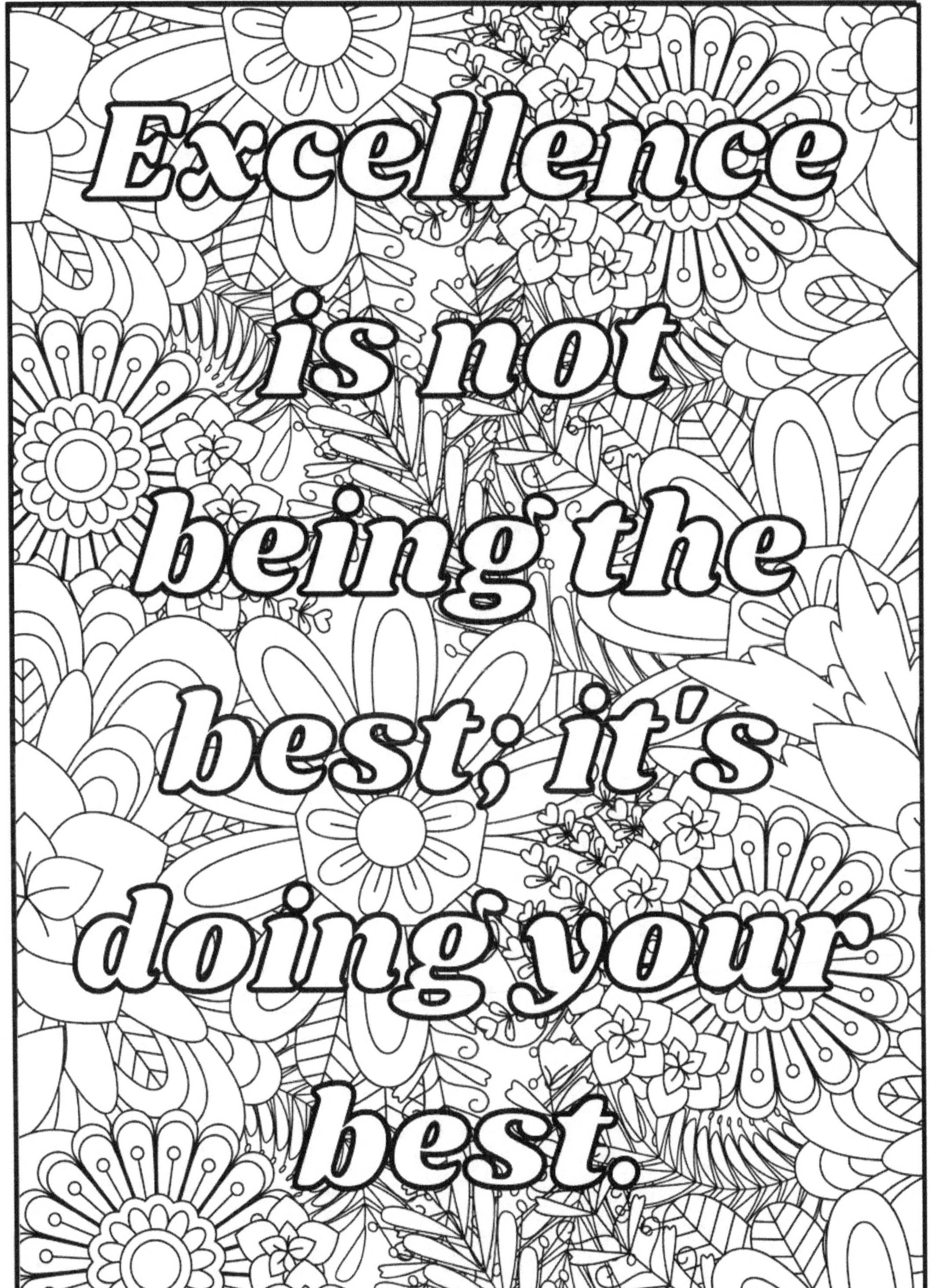

Excellence is not being the best; it's doing your best.

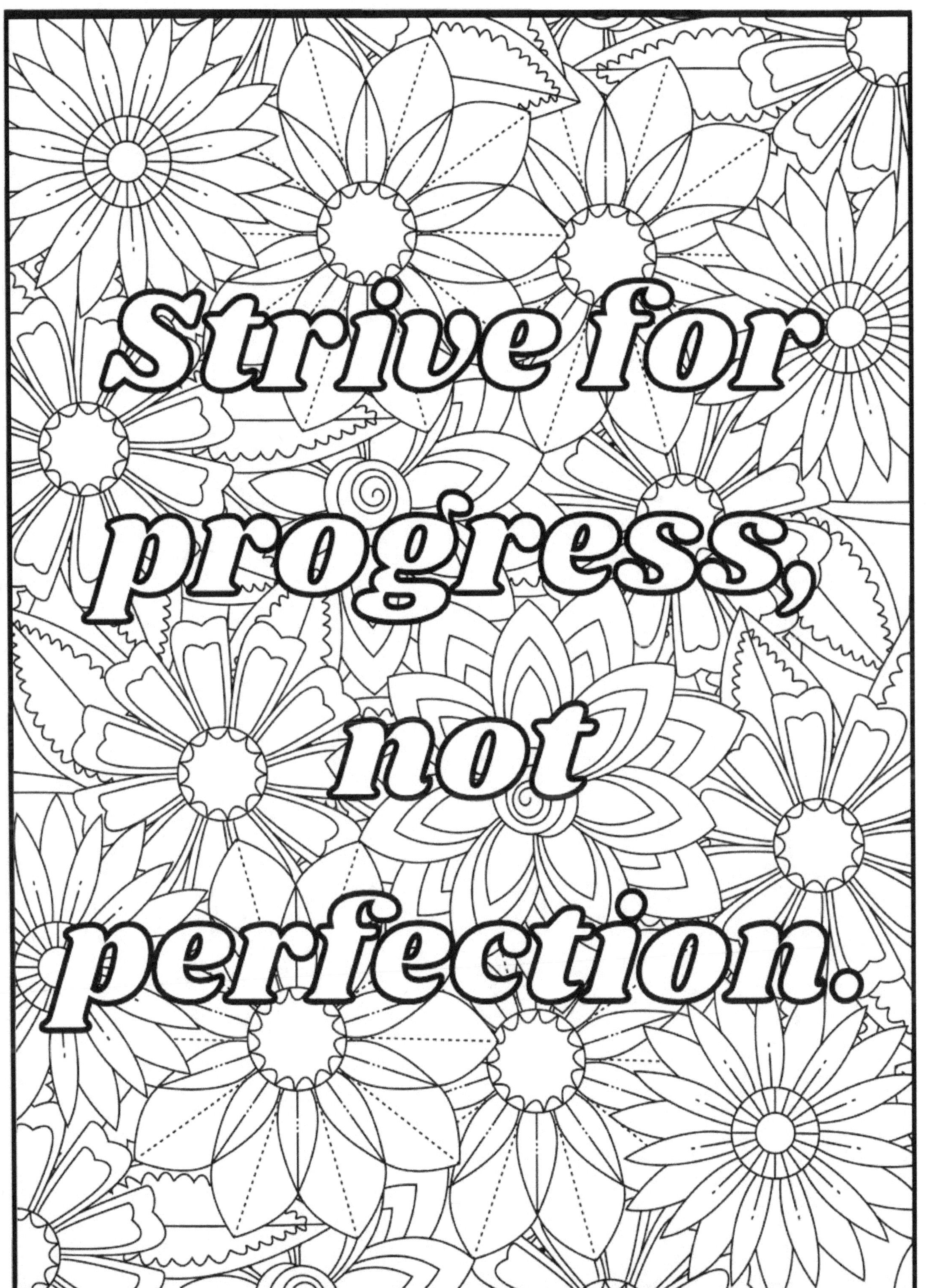
Strive for progress, not perfection.

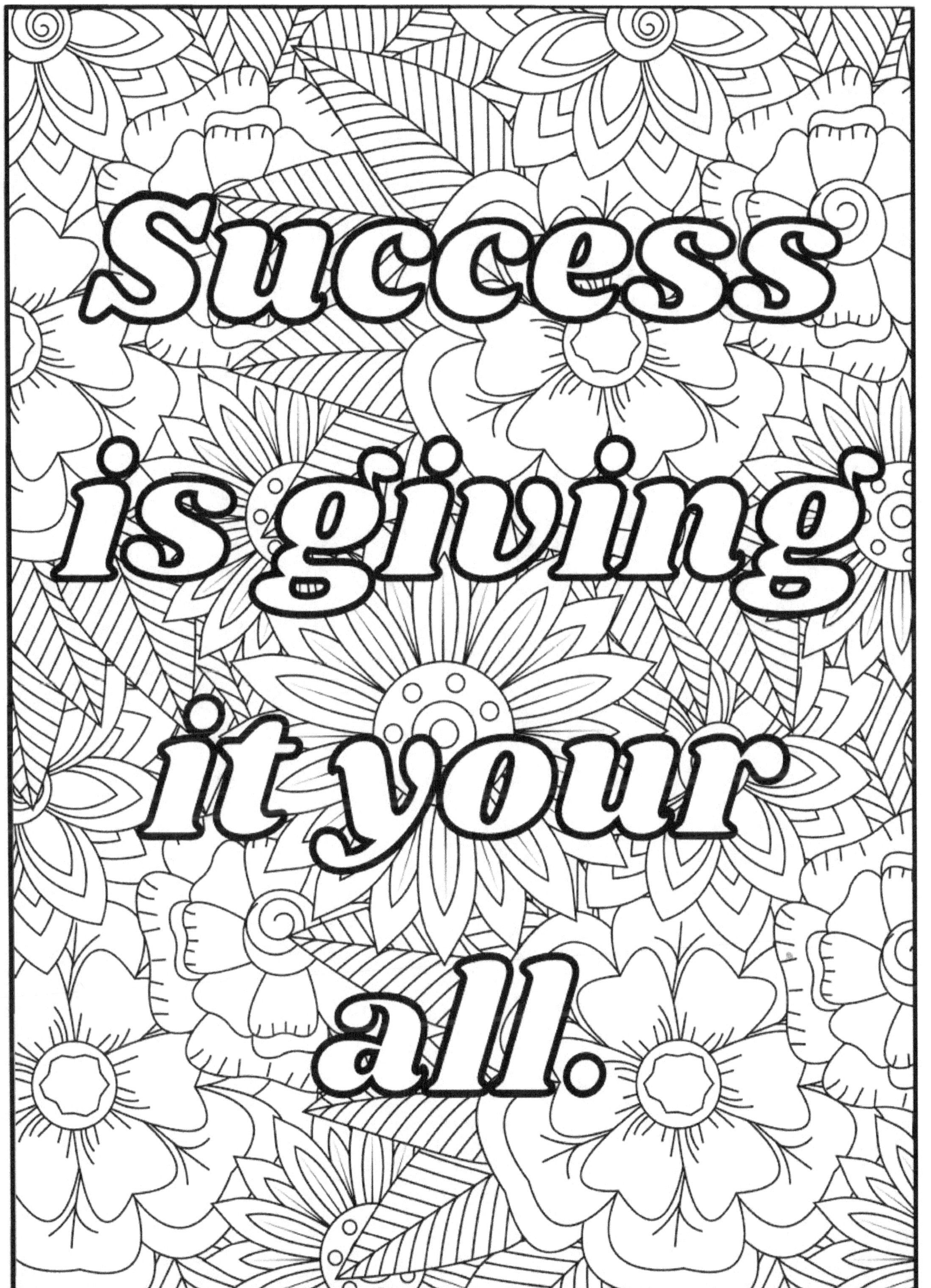

Success
is giving
it your
all.

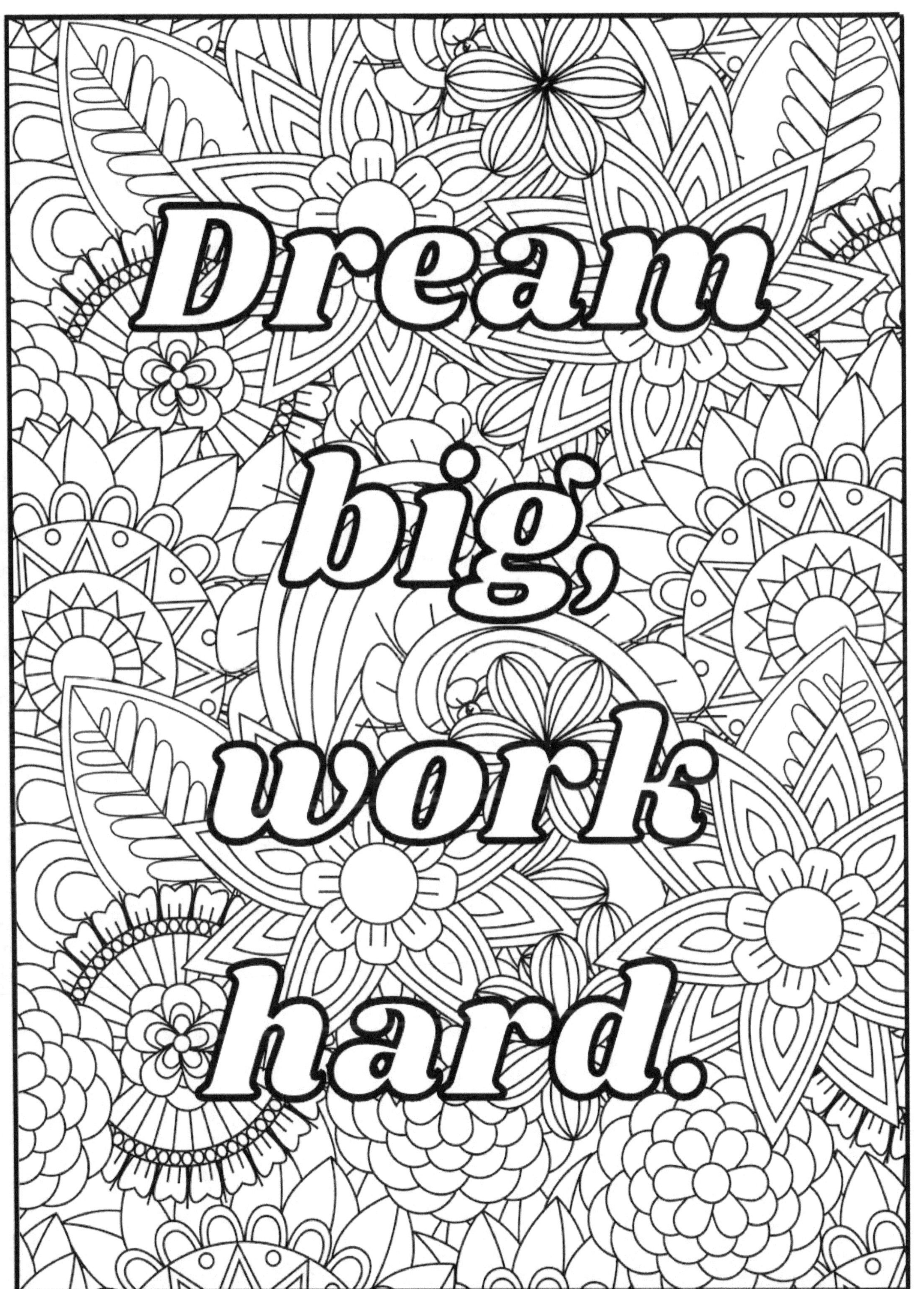

Dream
big,
work
hard.

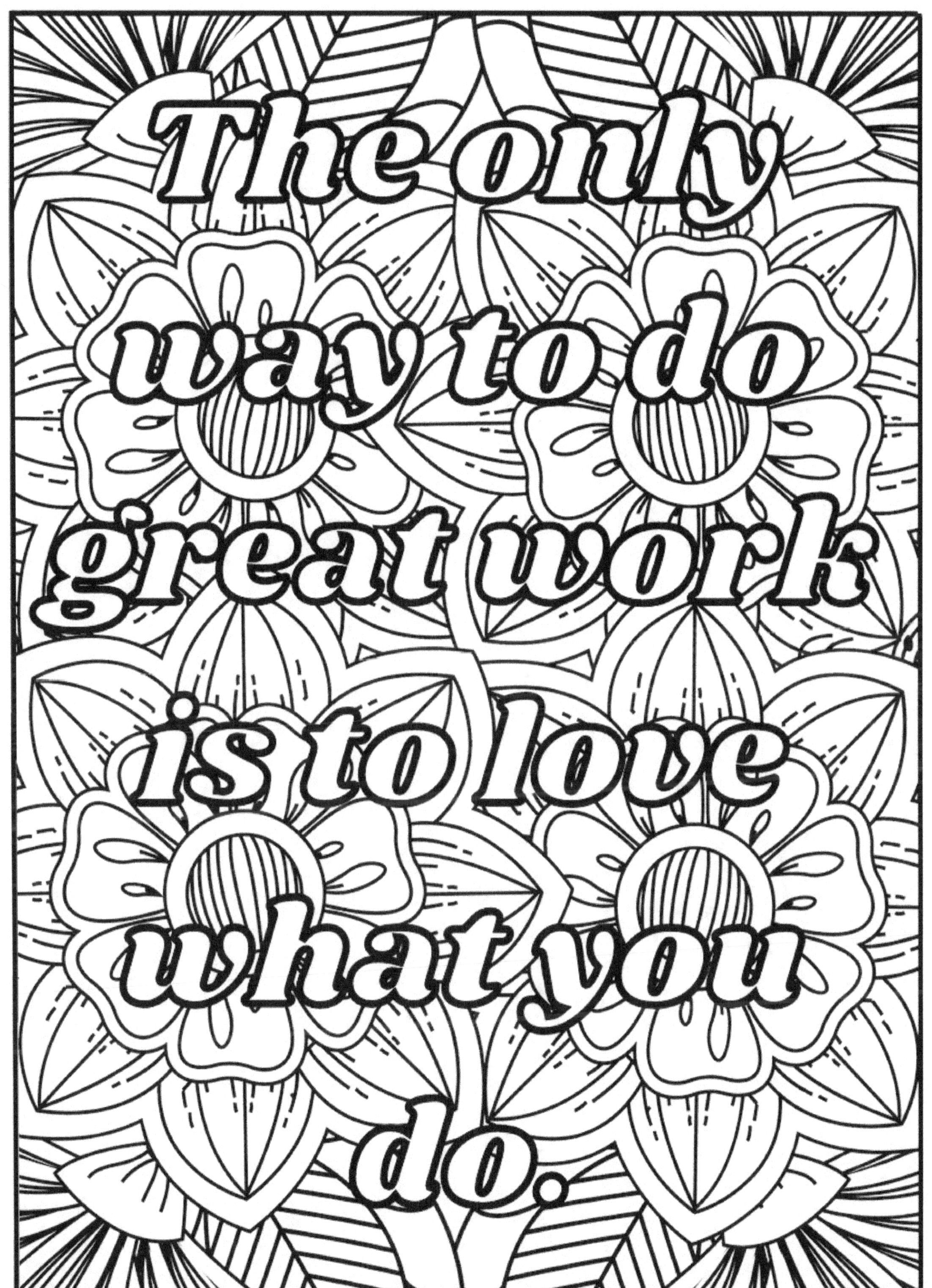

The only
way to do
great work
is to love
what you
do.

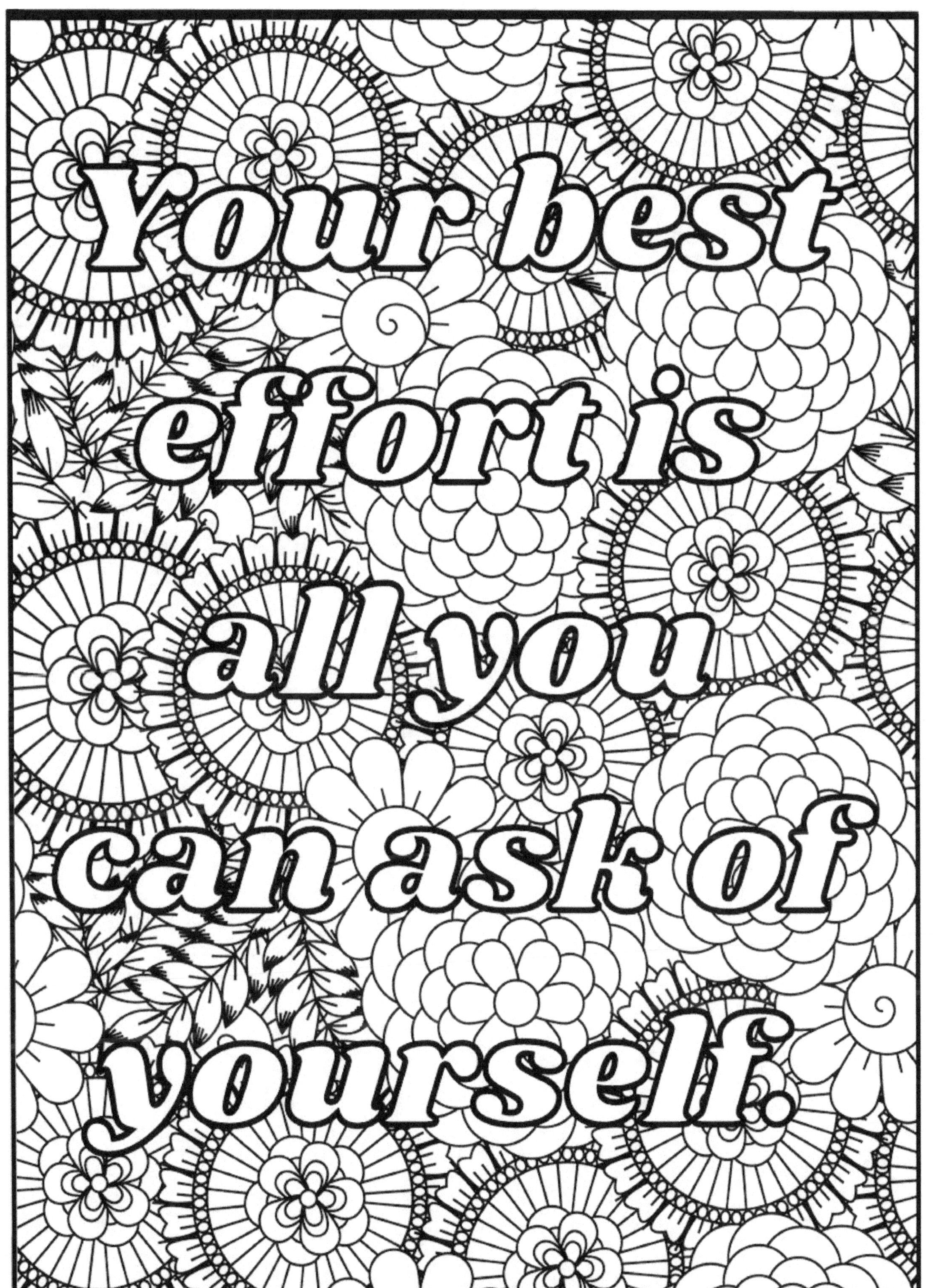
Your best effort is all you can ask of yourself.

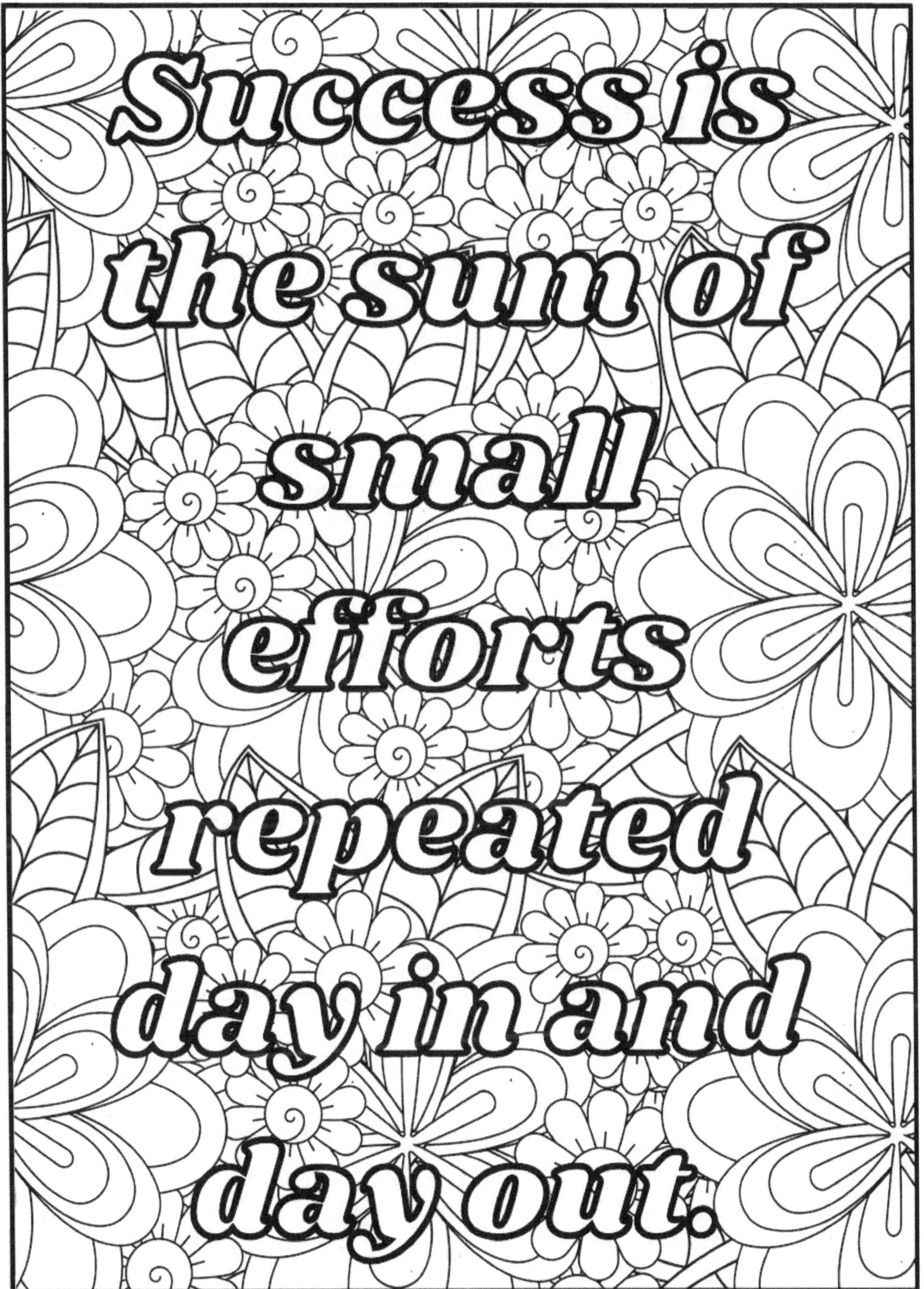

Success is
the sum of
small
efforts
repeated
day in and
day out.

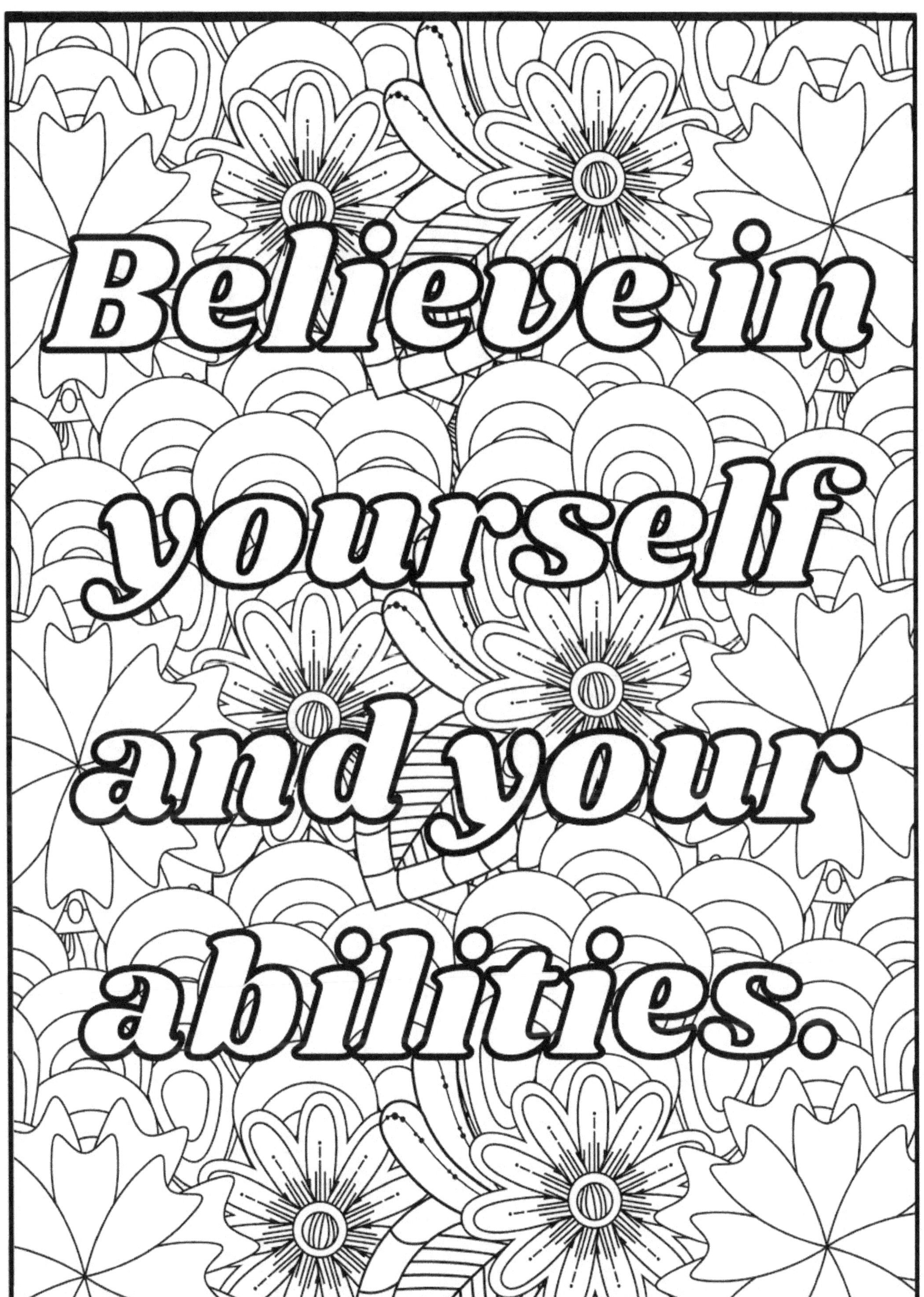

Believe in
yourself
and your
abilities.

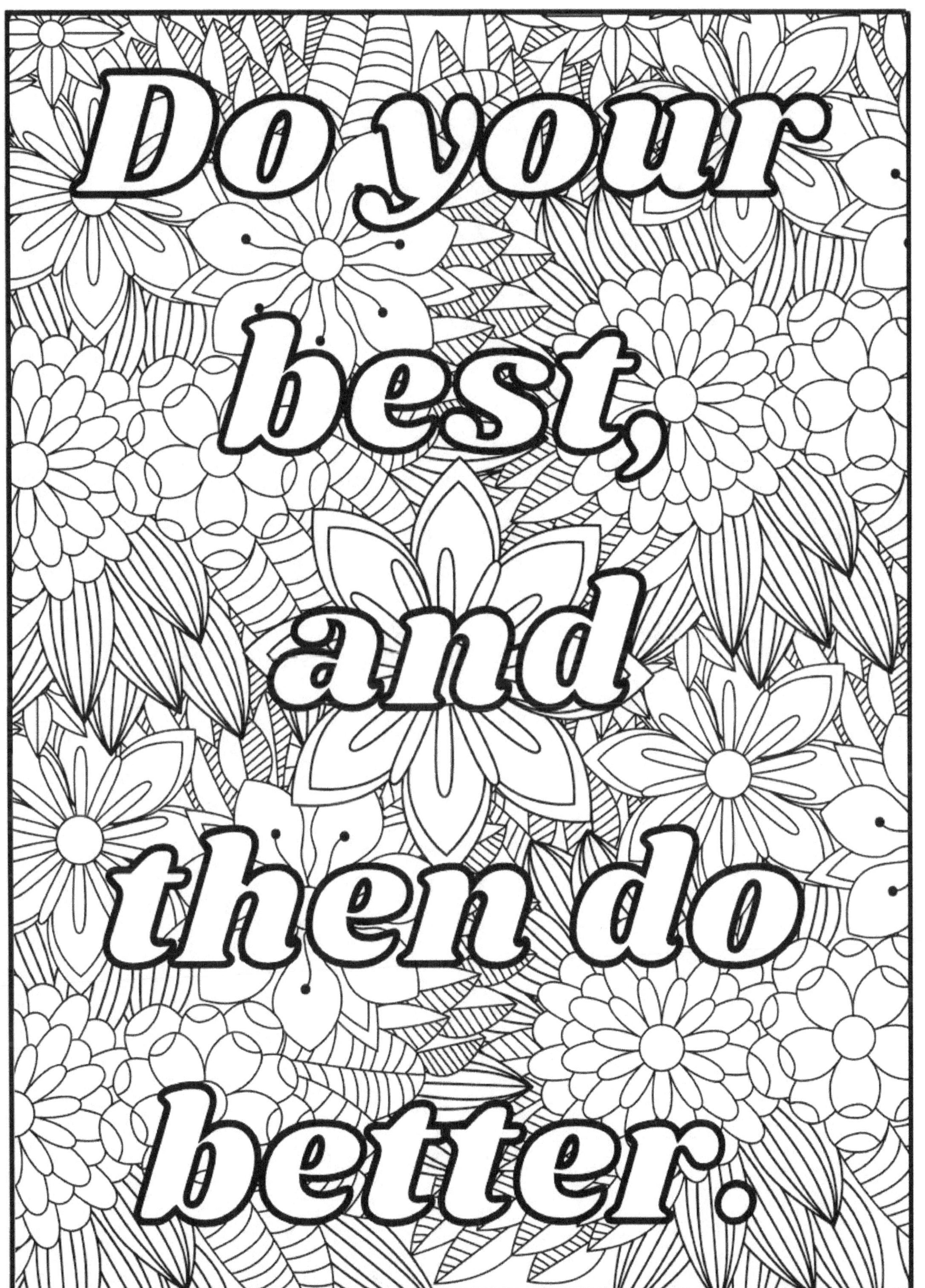
Do your
best,
and
then do
better.

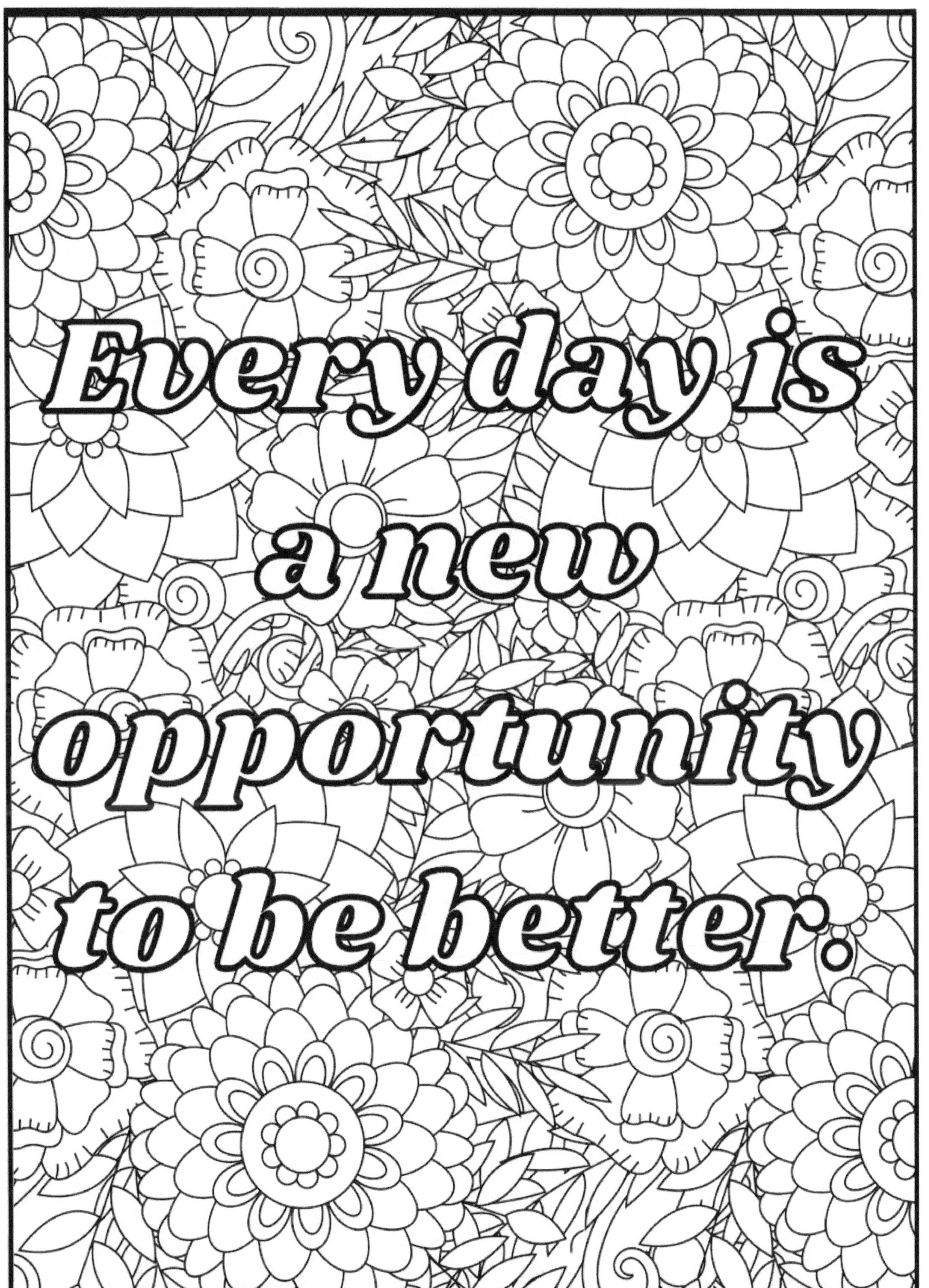

Every day is
a new
opportunity
to be better.

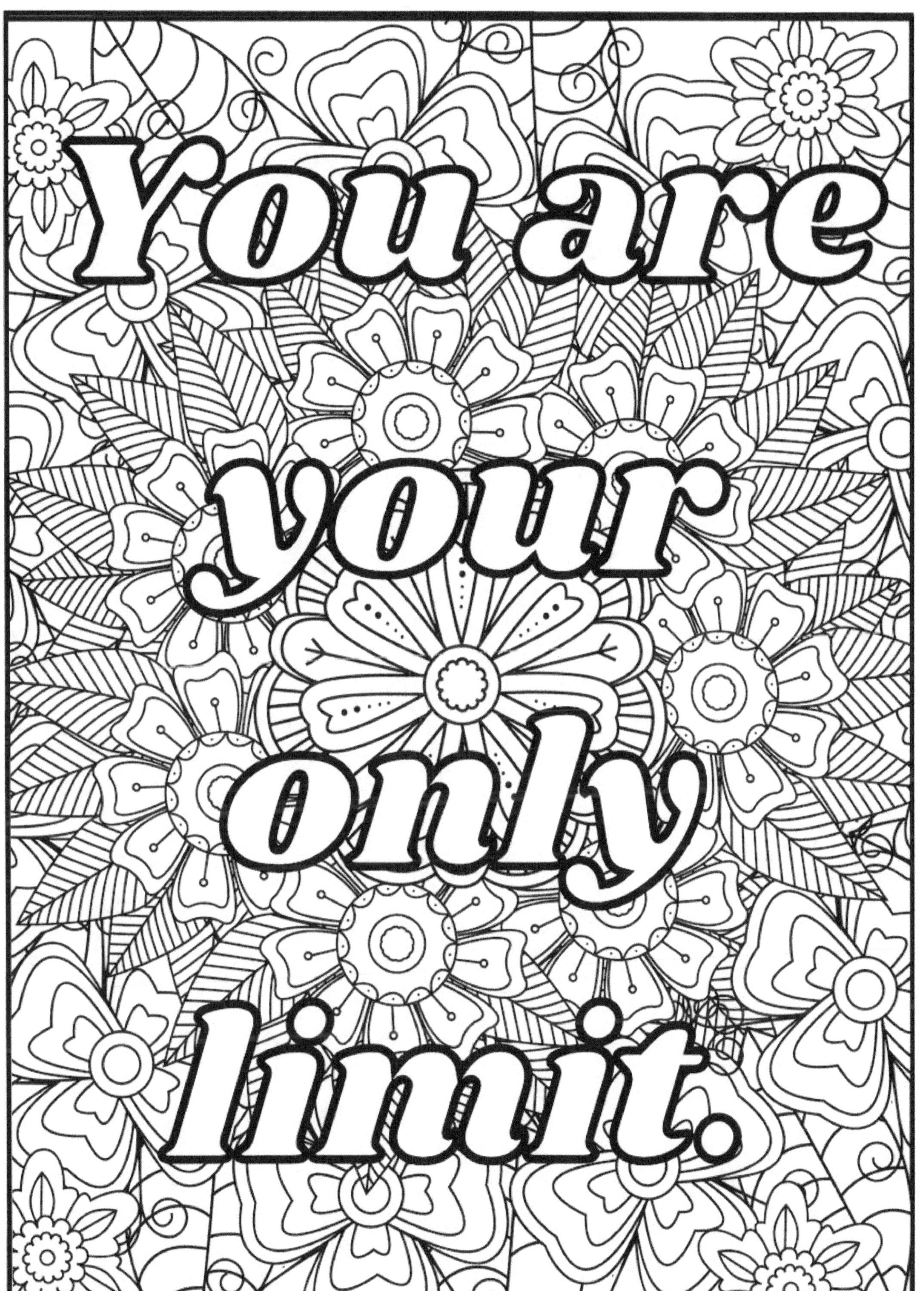

You are
your
only
limit.

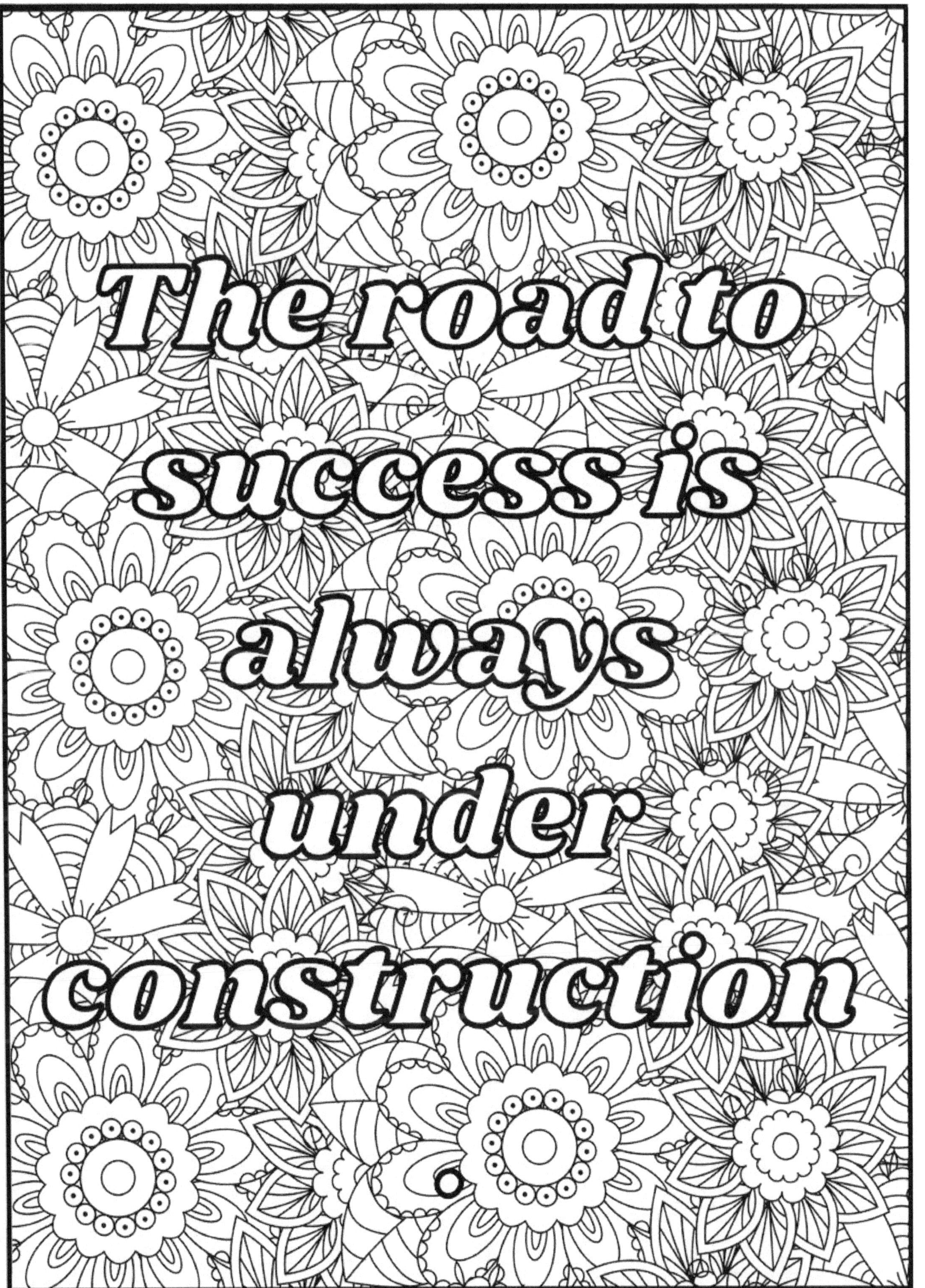
The road to
success is
always
under
construction

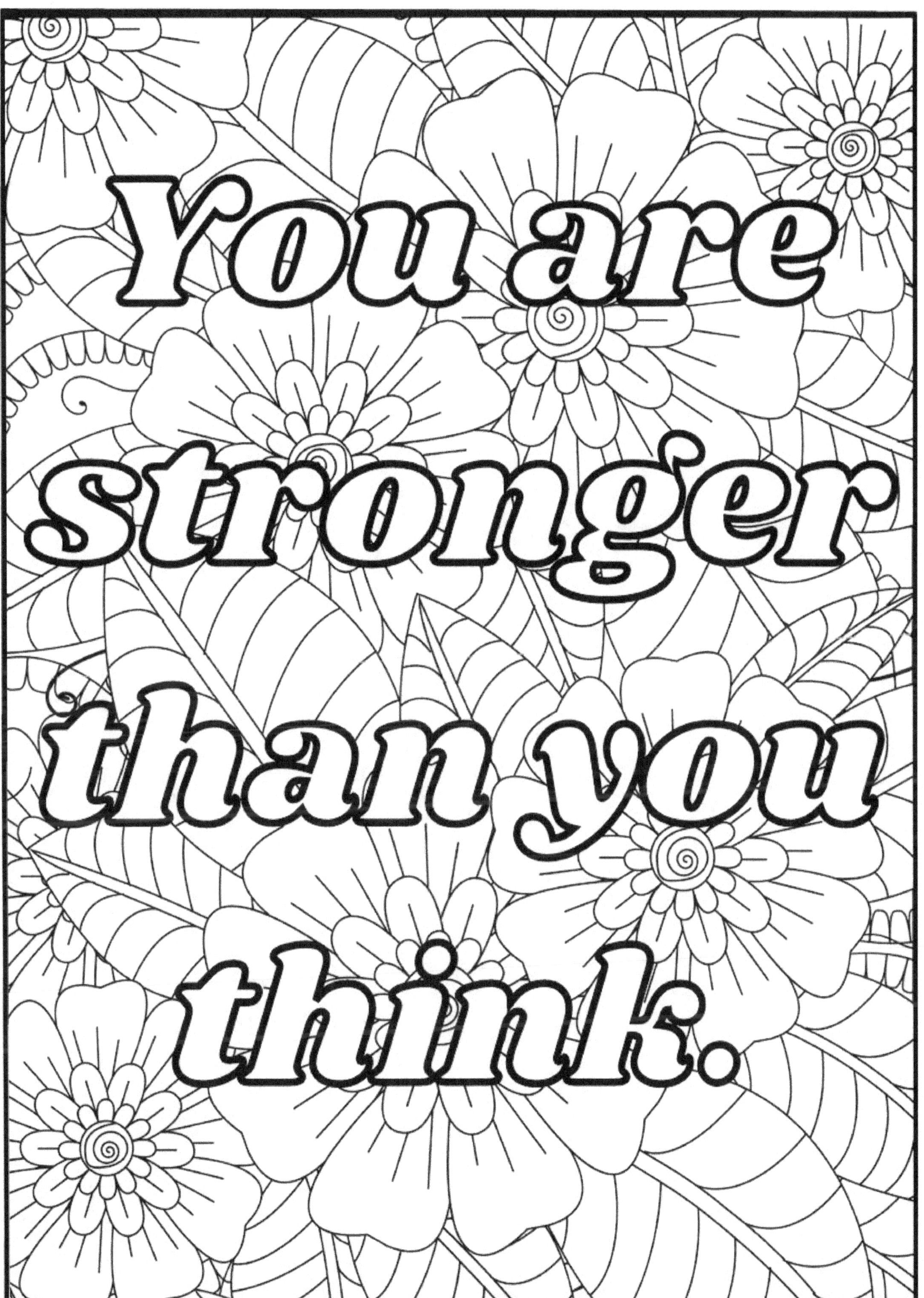
You are stronger than you think.

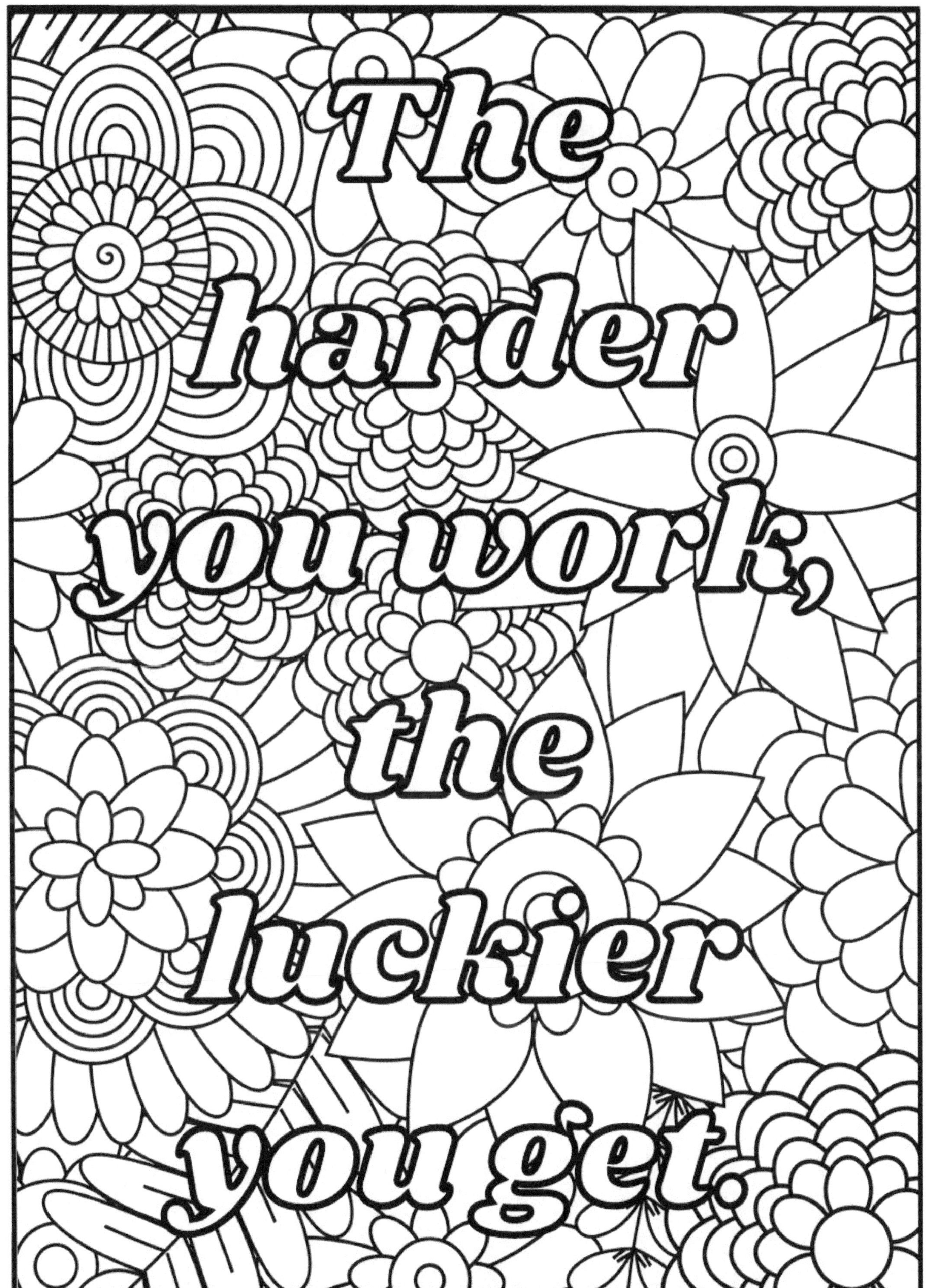

The harder you work, the luckier you get.

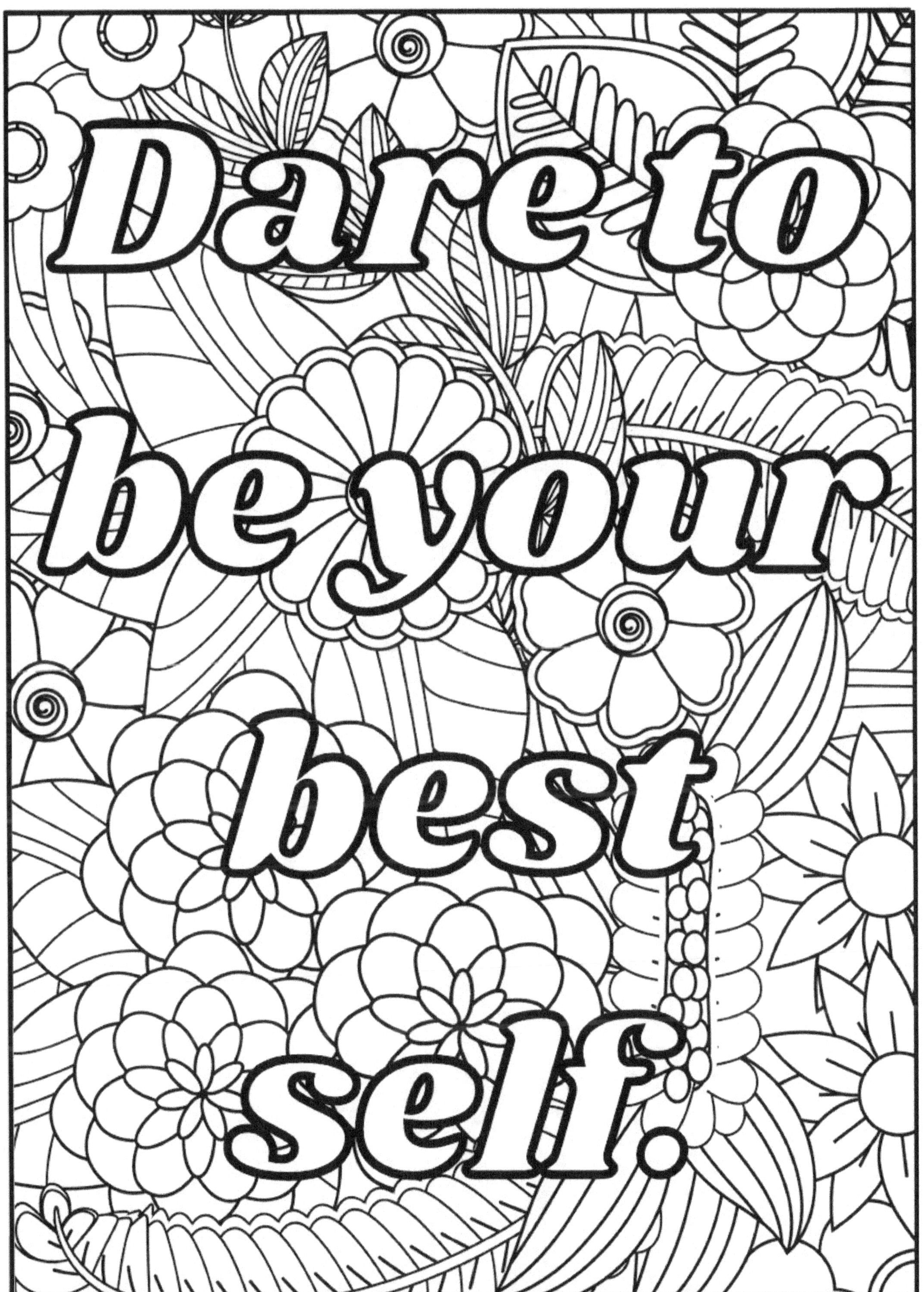

Dare to
be your
best
self.

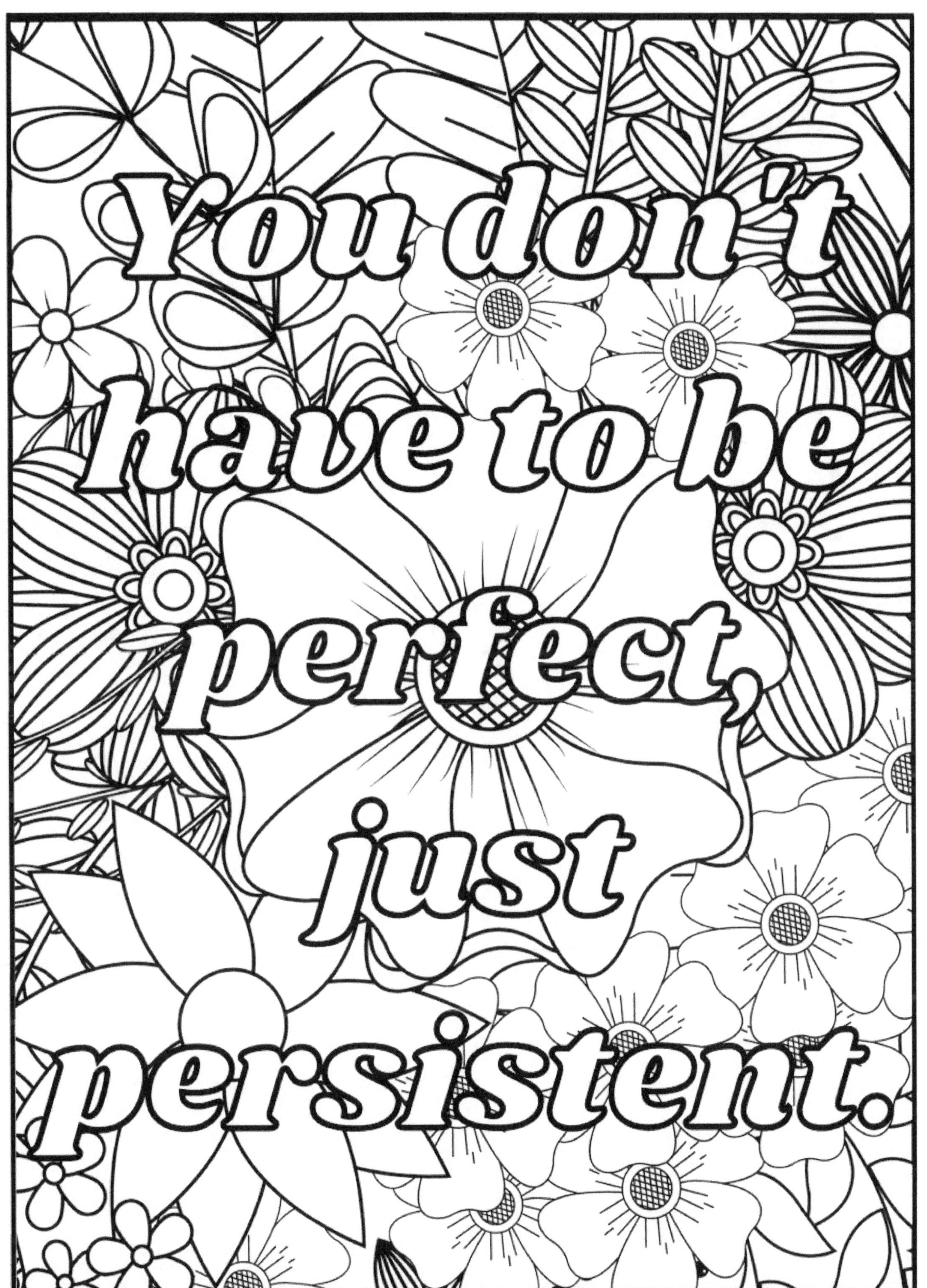
You don't
have to be
perfect,
just
persistent.

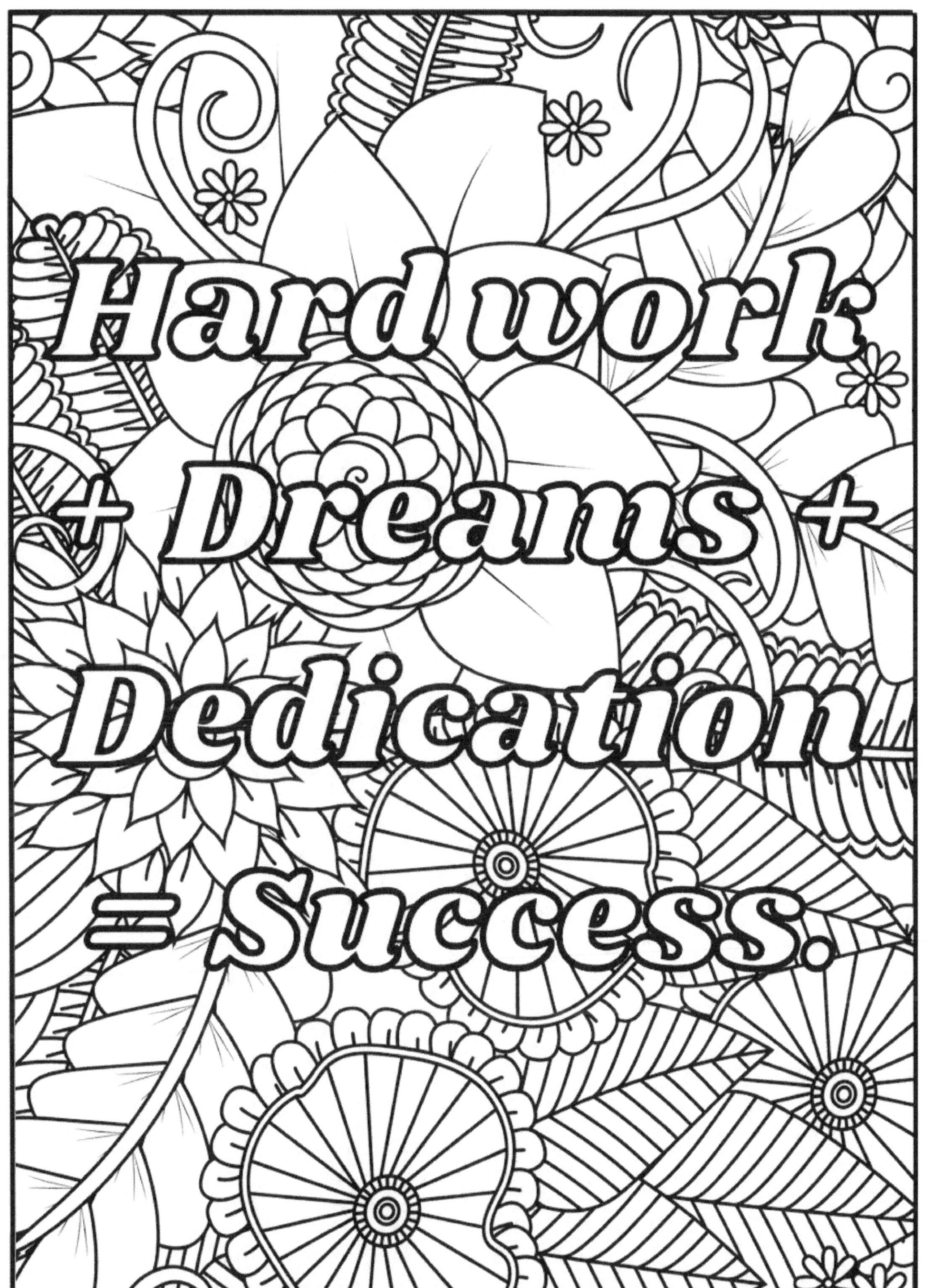

Hard work
+ Dreams +
Dedication
= Success.

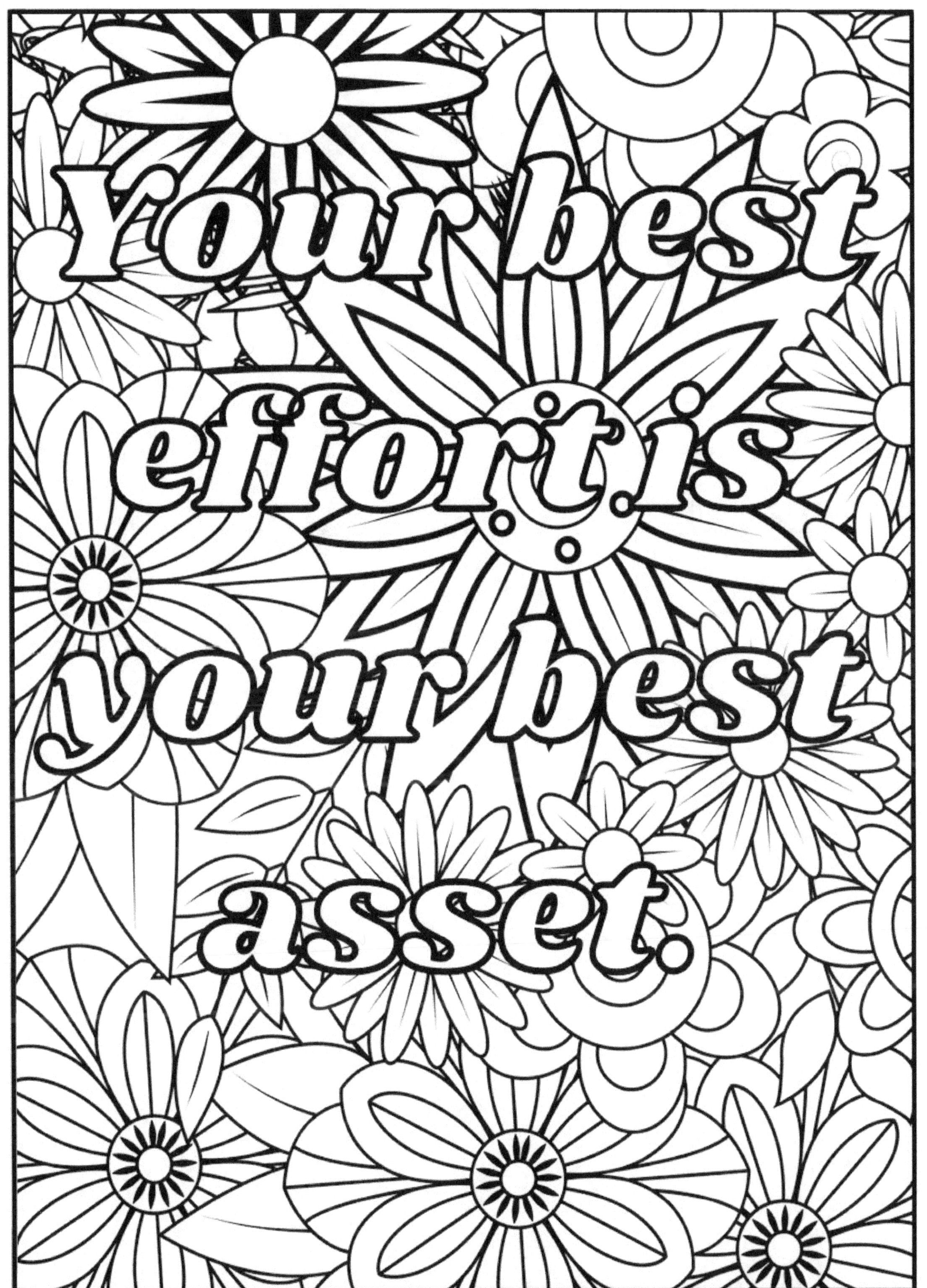

Your best
effort is
your best
asset.

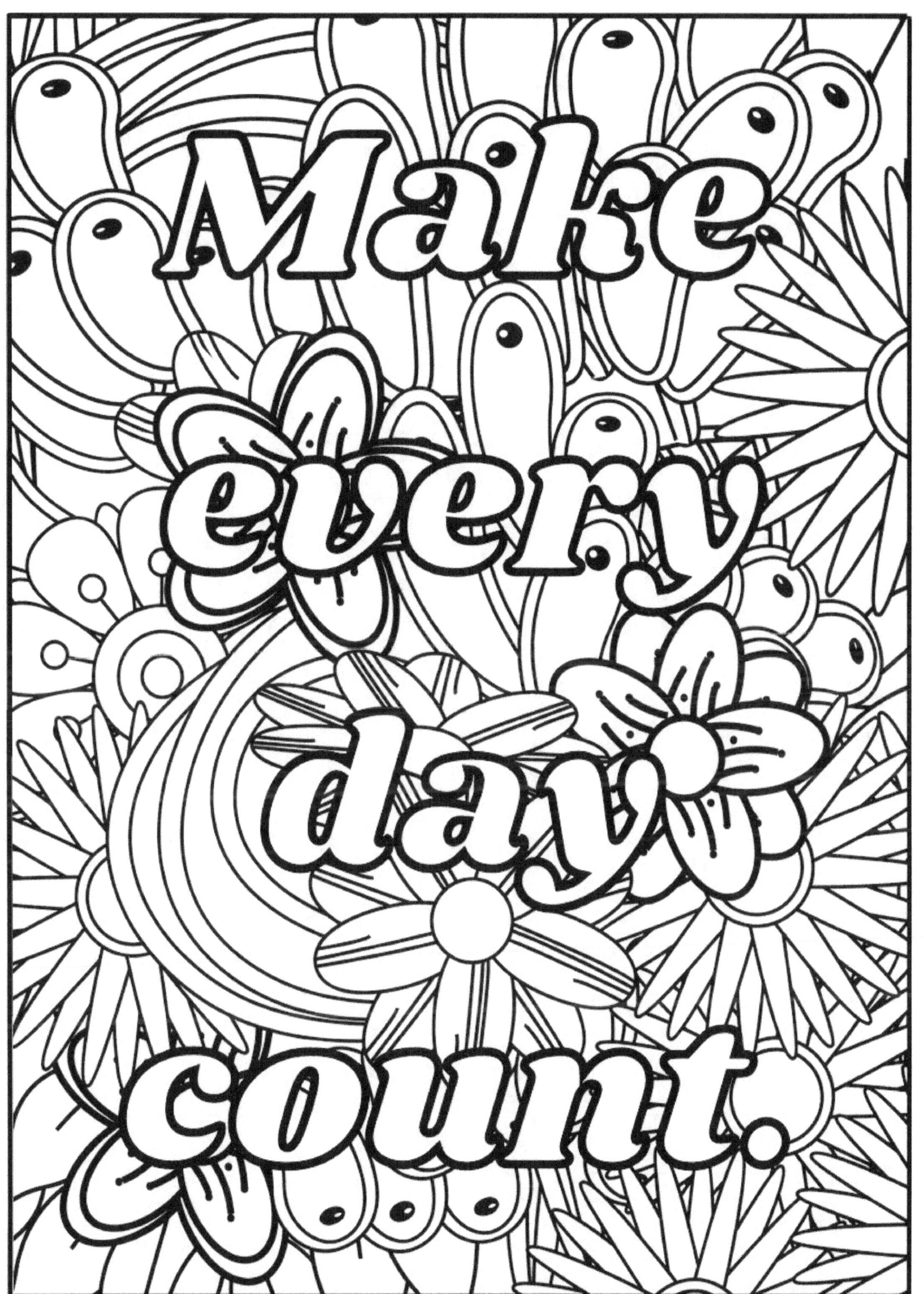
Make
every
day
count.

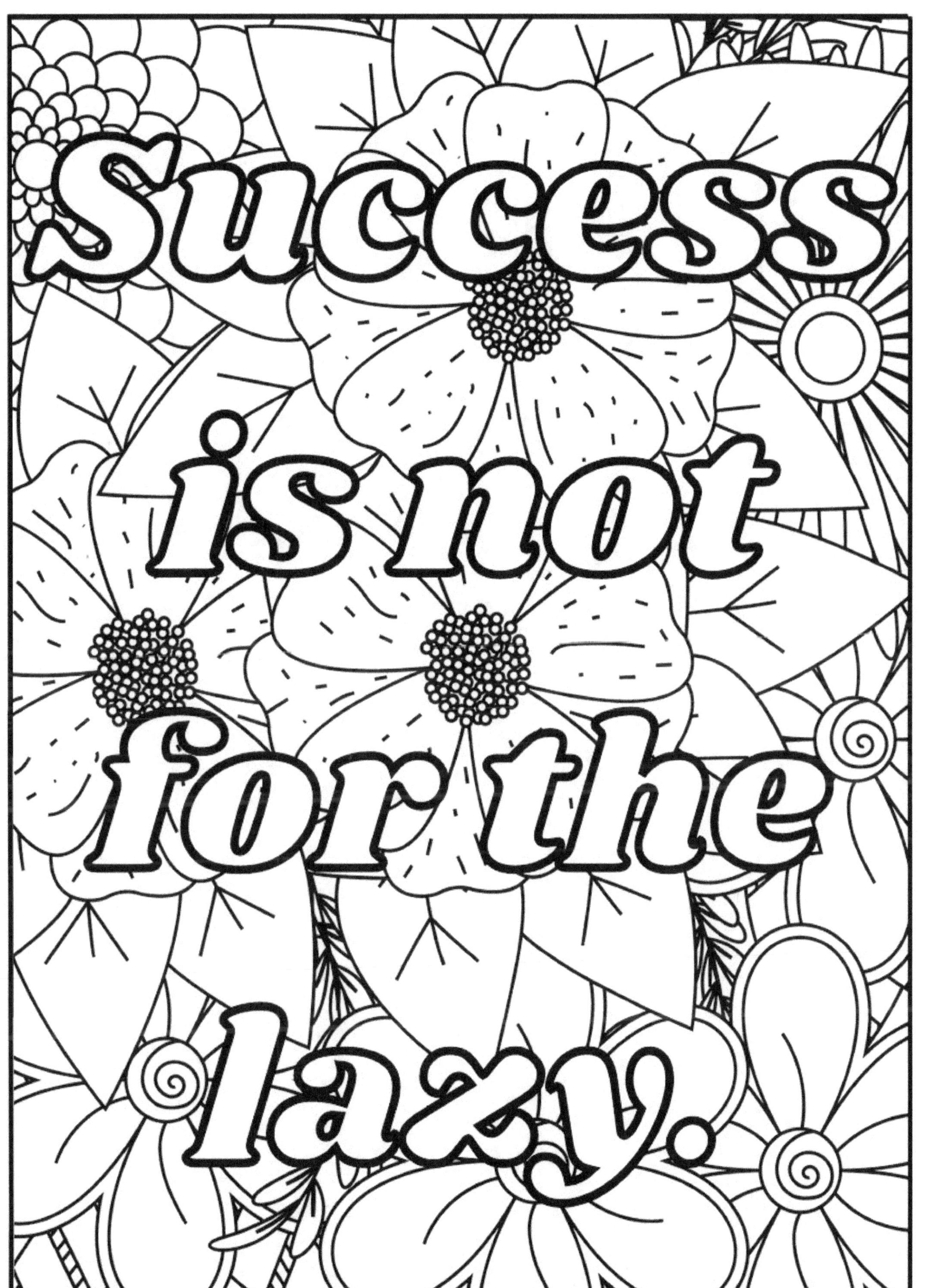
Success is not for the lazy.

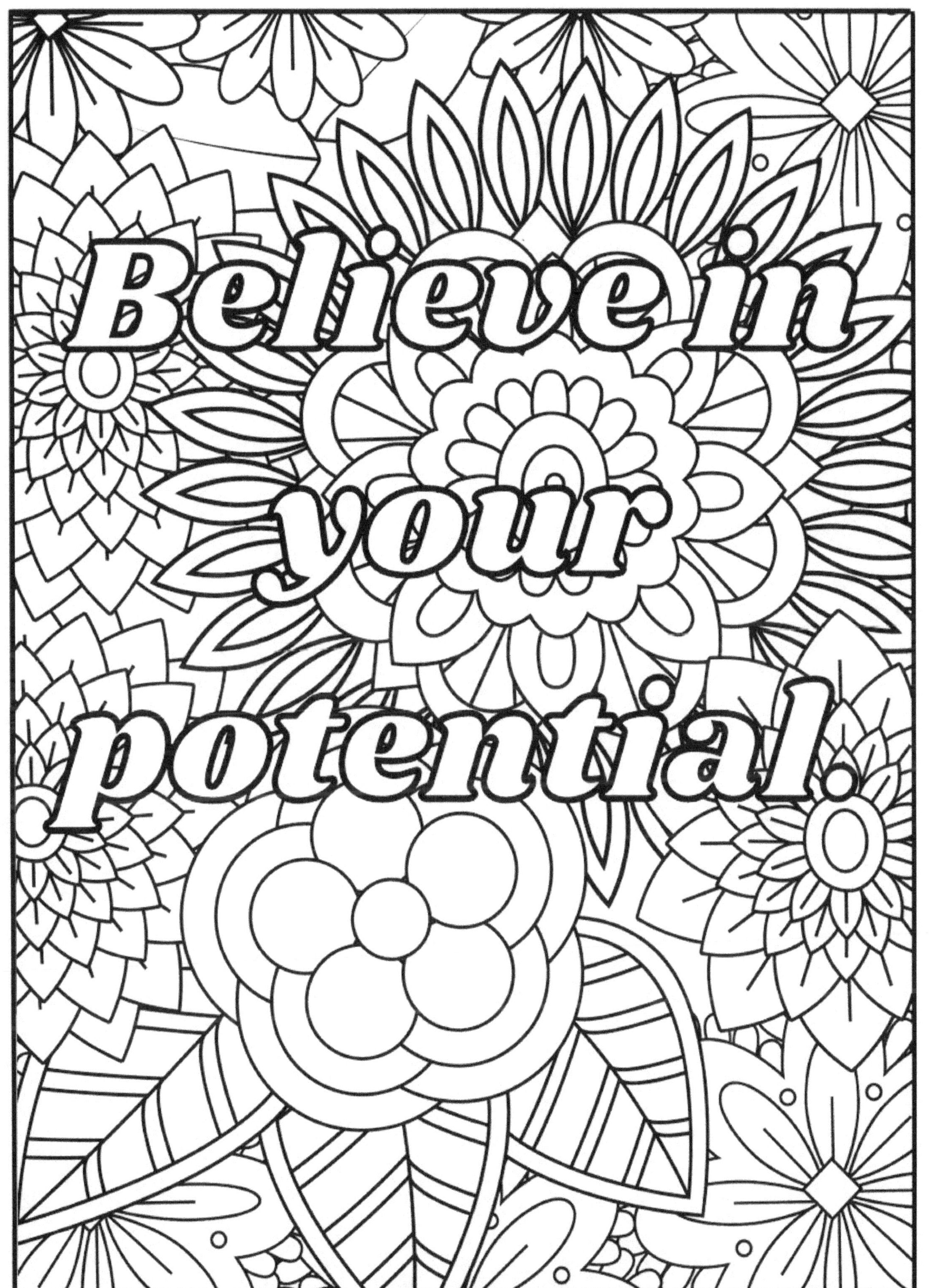

Believe in
your
potential.

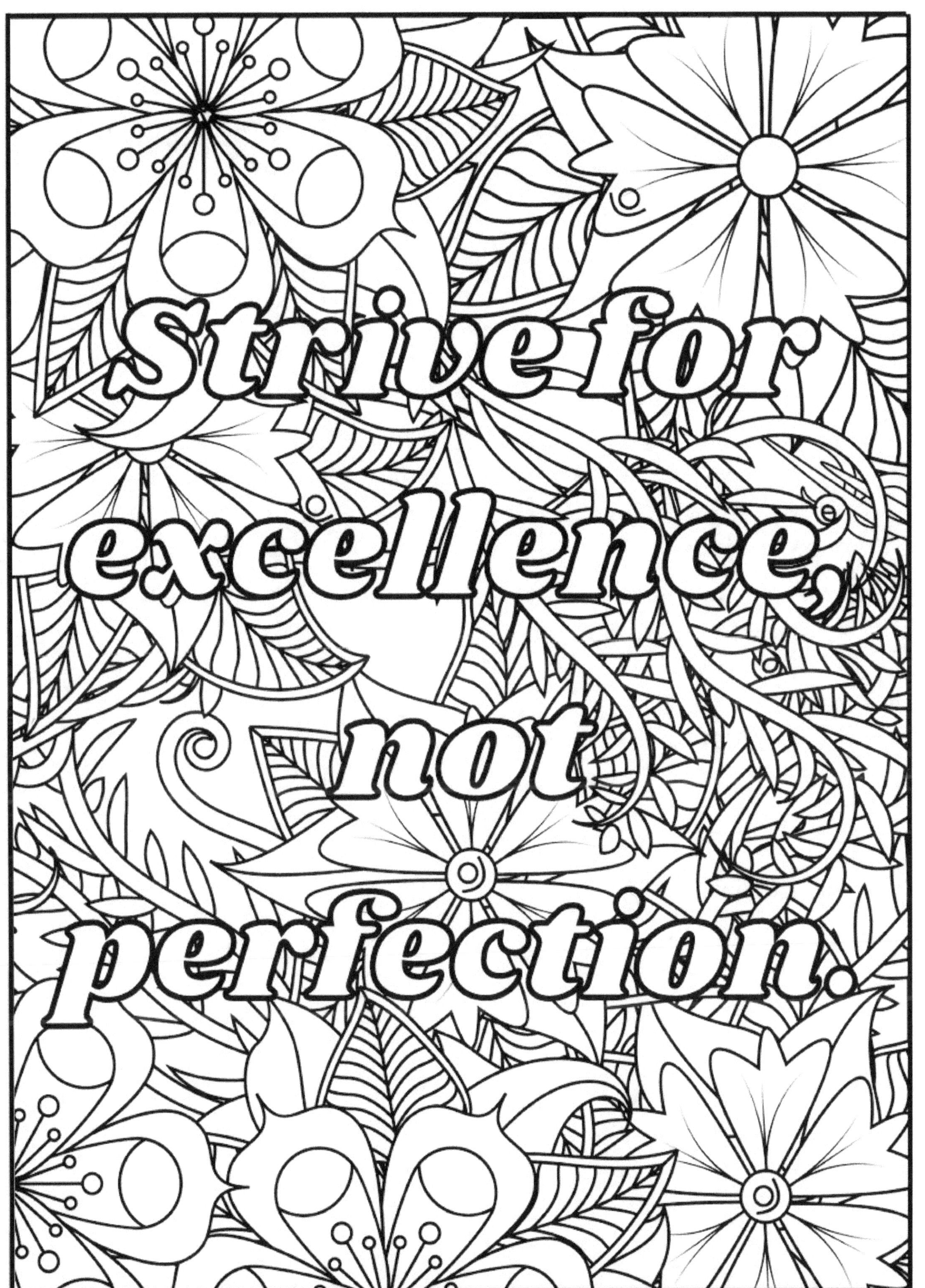

Strive for excellence, not perfection.

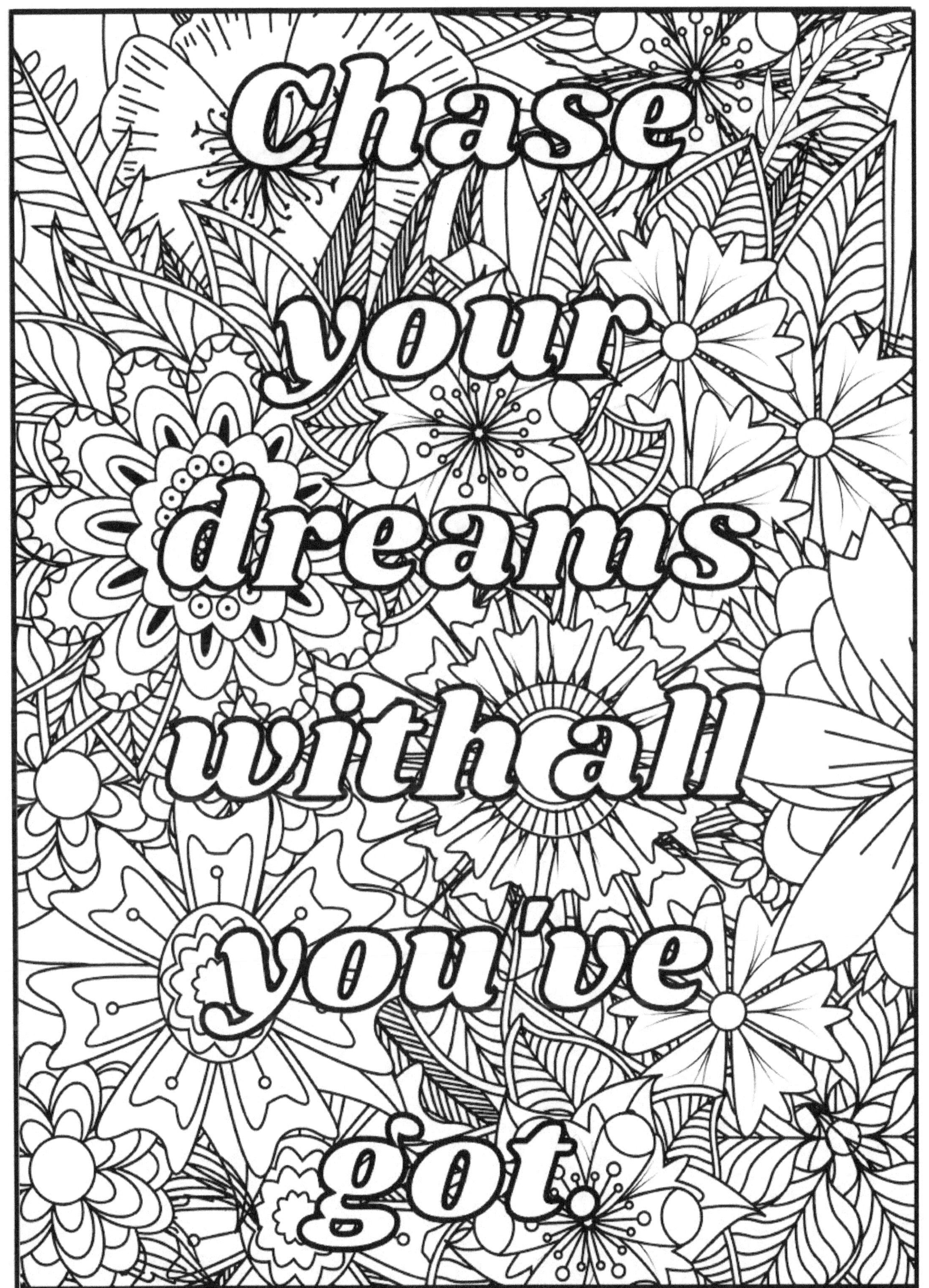

Chase
your
dreams
withall
you've
got.

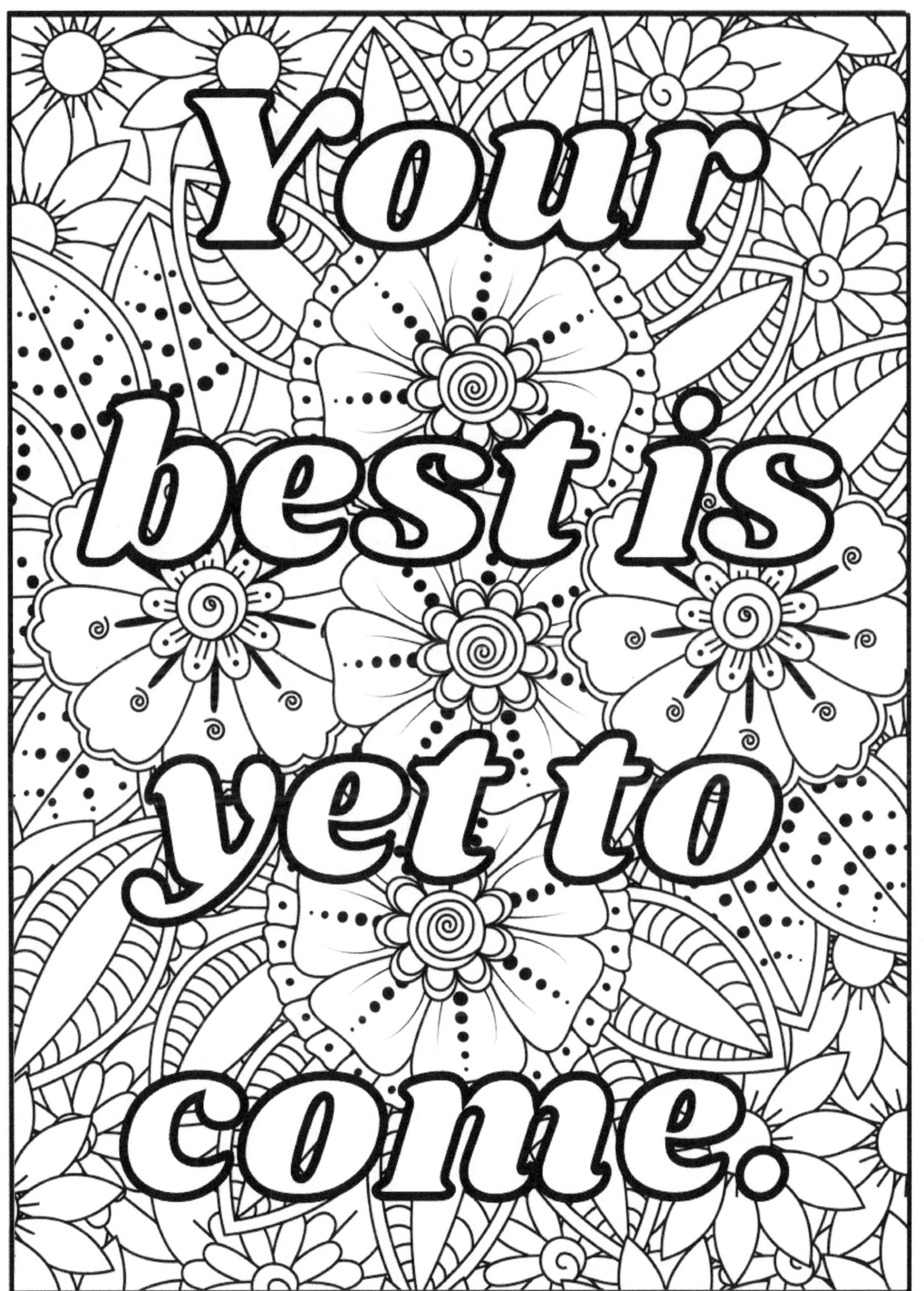

Your
best is
yet to
come.

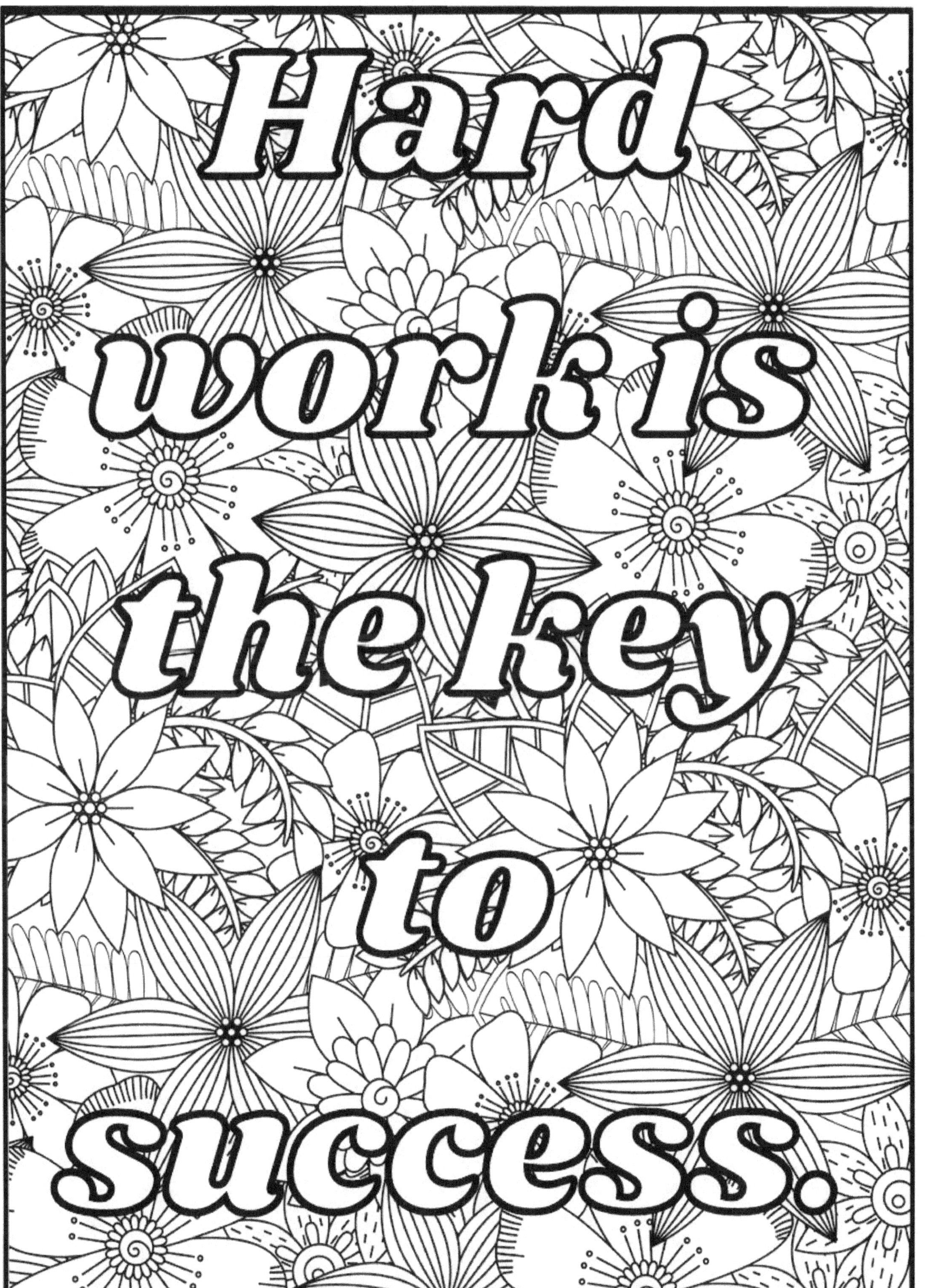

Hard
work is
the key
to
success.

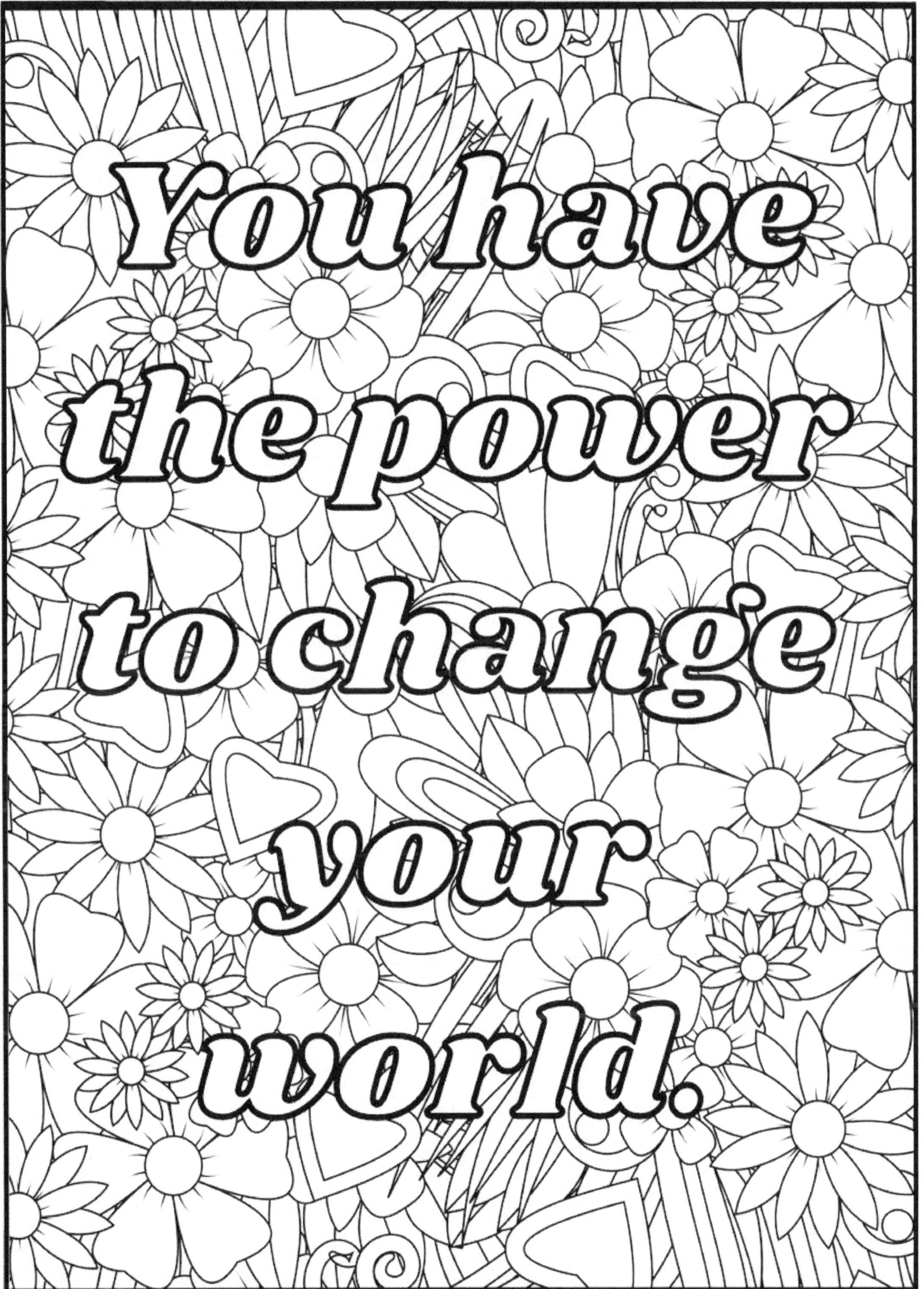

You have
the power
to change
your
world.

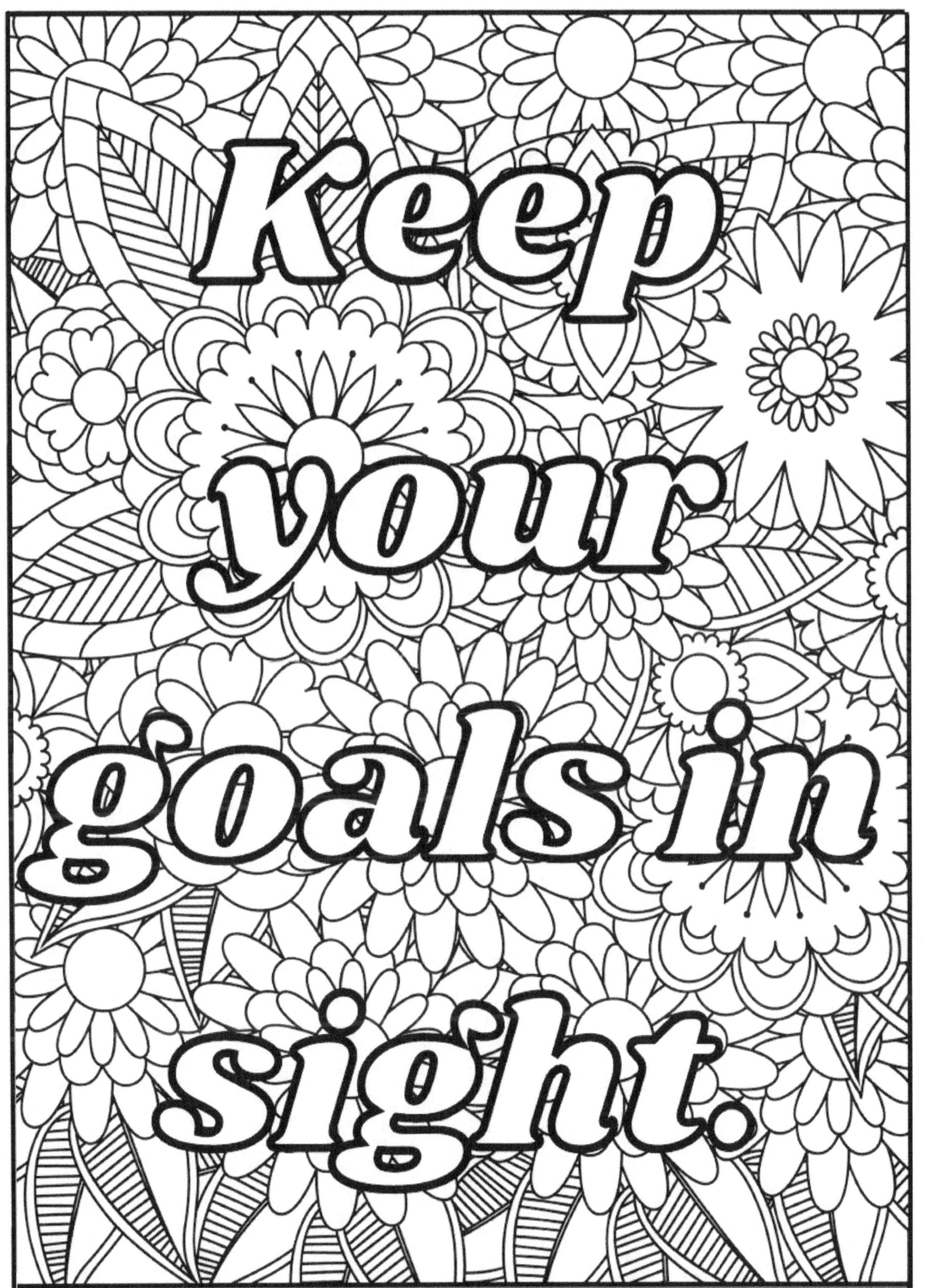

Keep
your
goals in
sight.

Success is earned, not given.

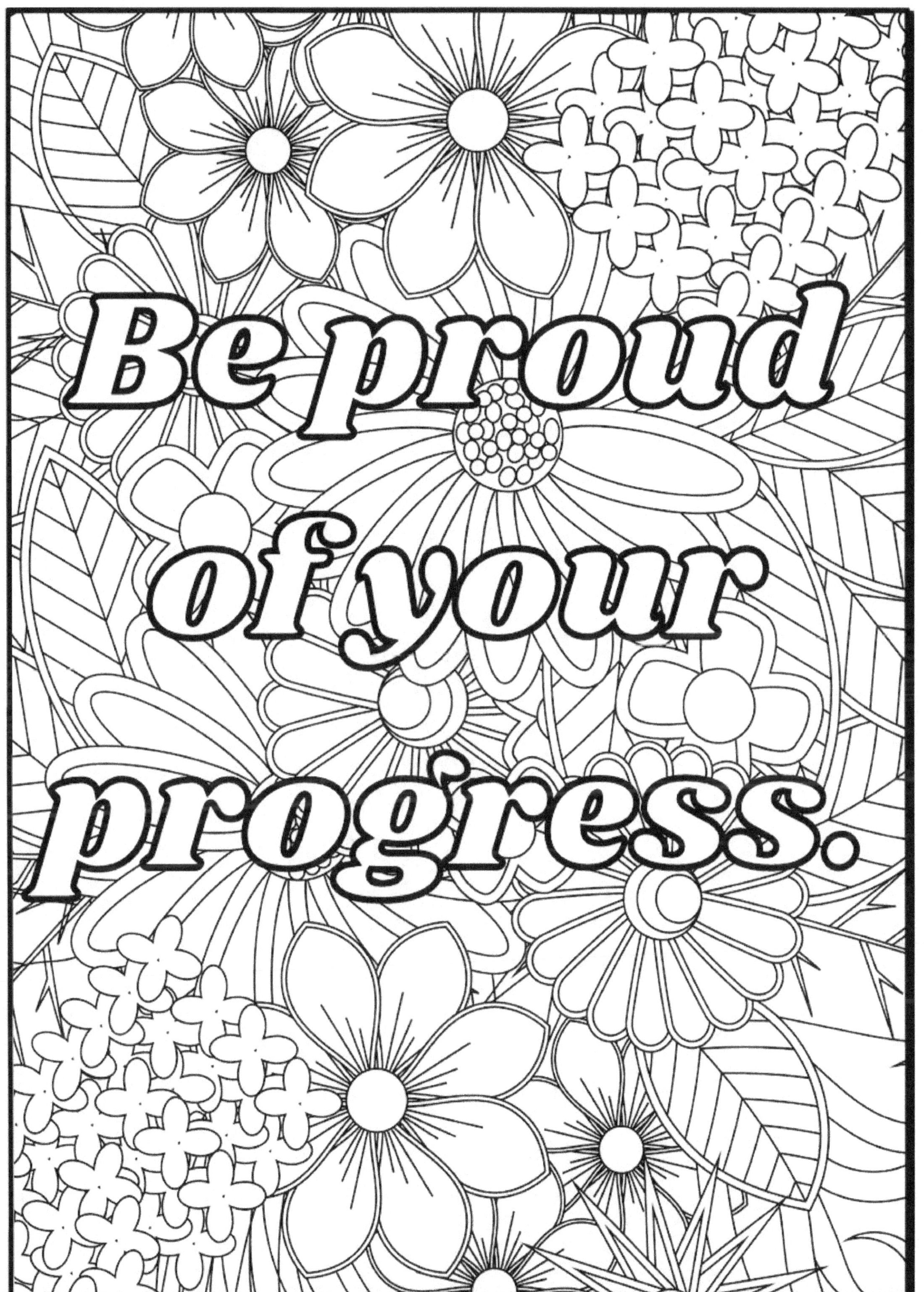

Be proud
of your
progress.

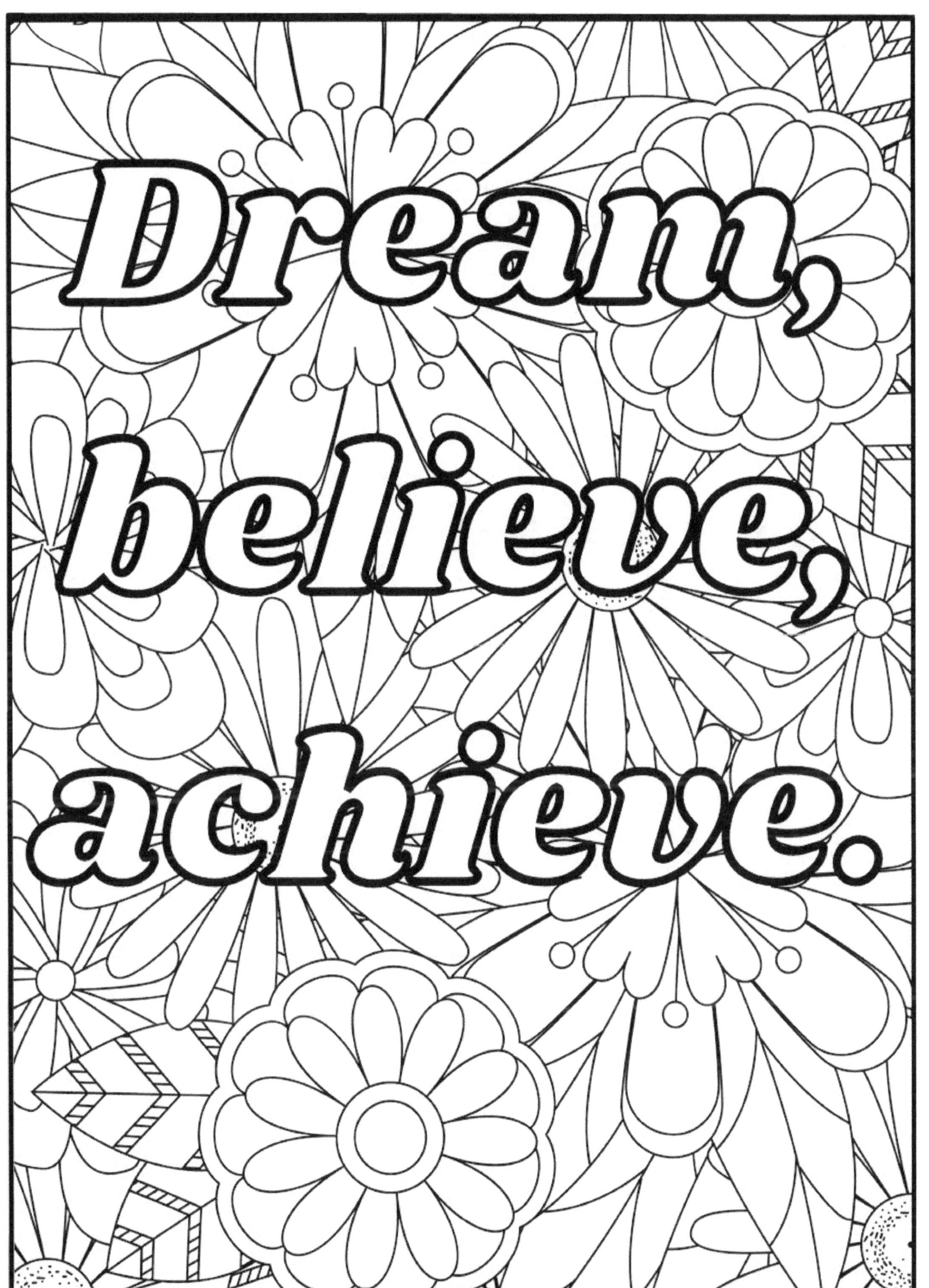

Dream,
believe,
achieve.

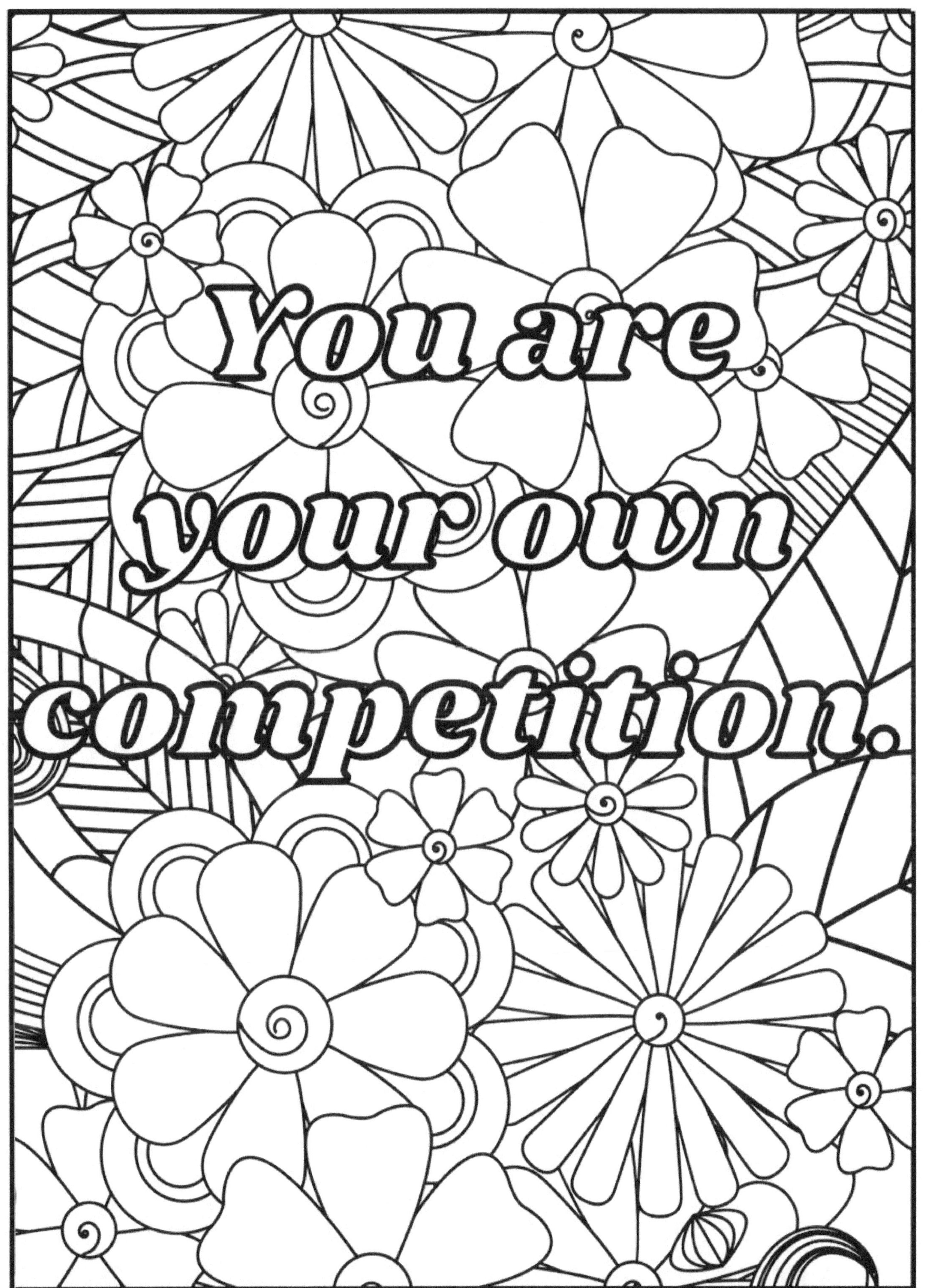

You are
your own
competition.

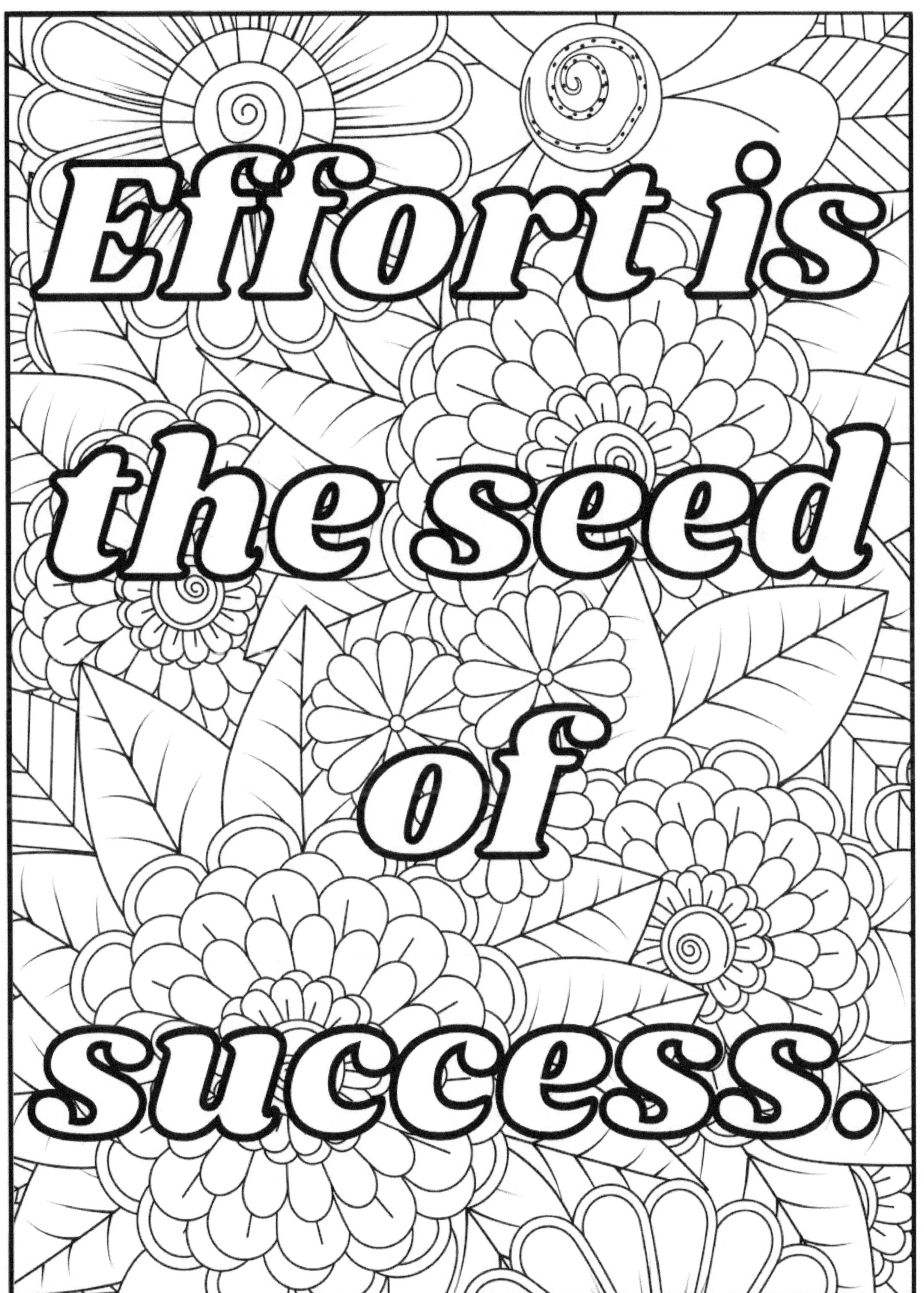

Effort is
the seed
of
success.

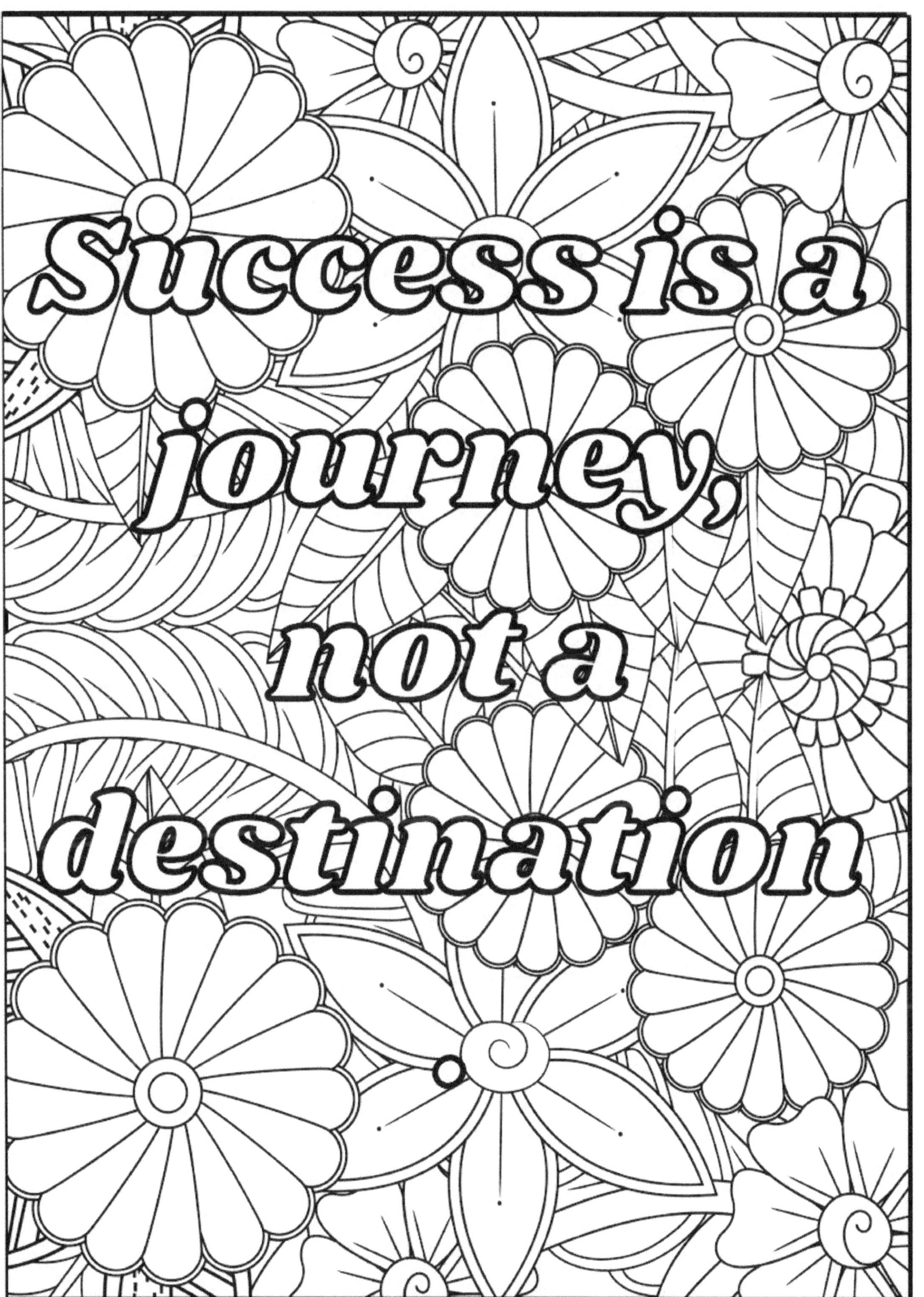
Success is a journey, not a destination

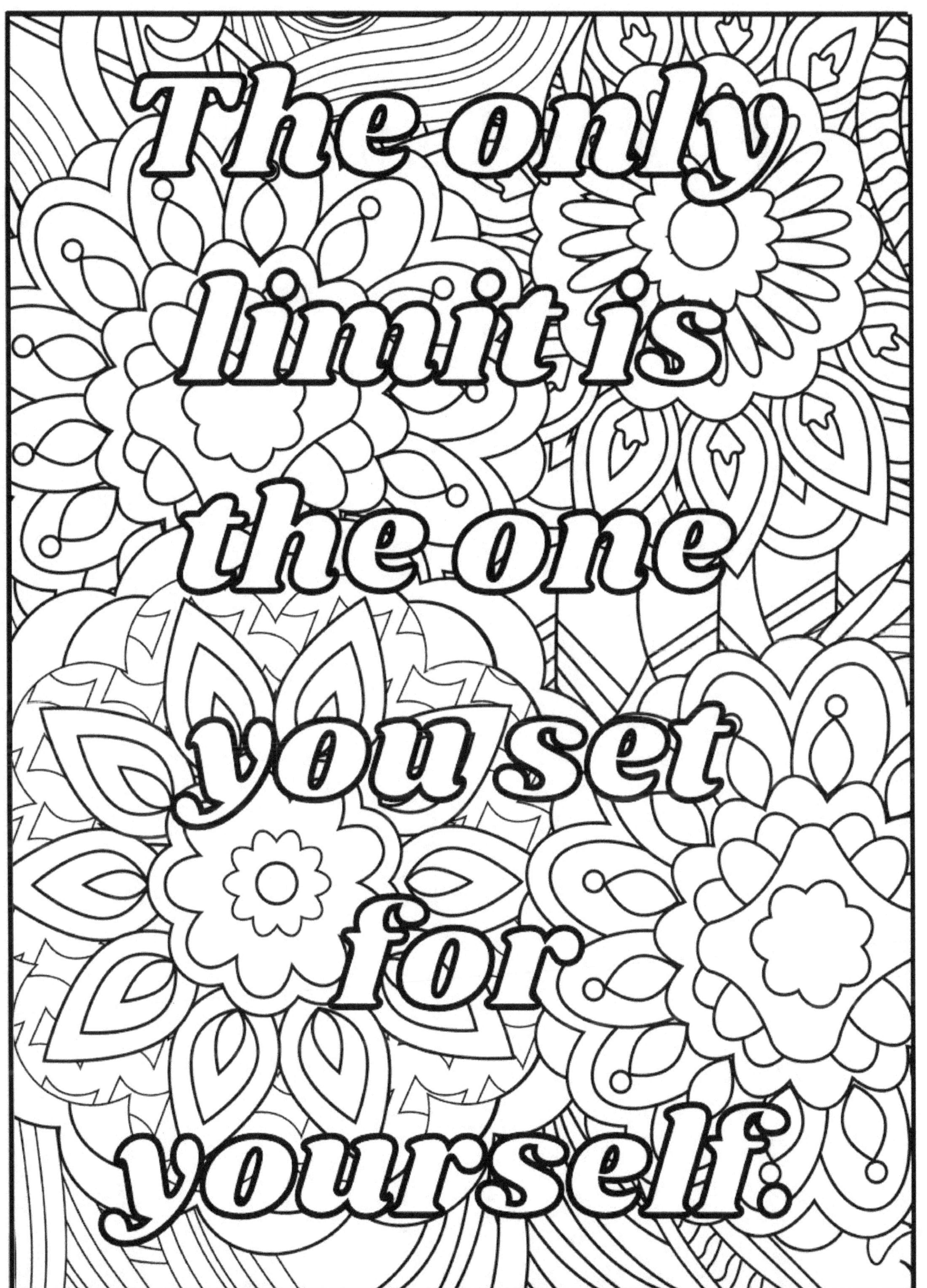

The only limit is the one you set for yourself.

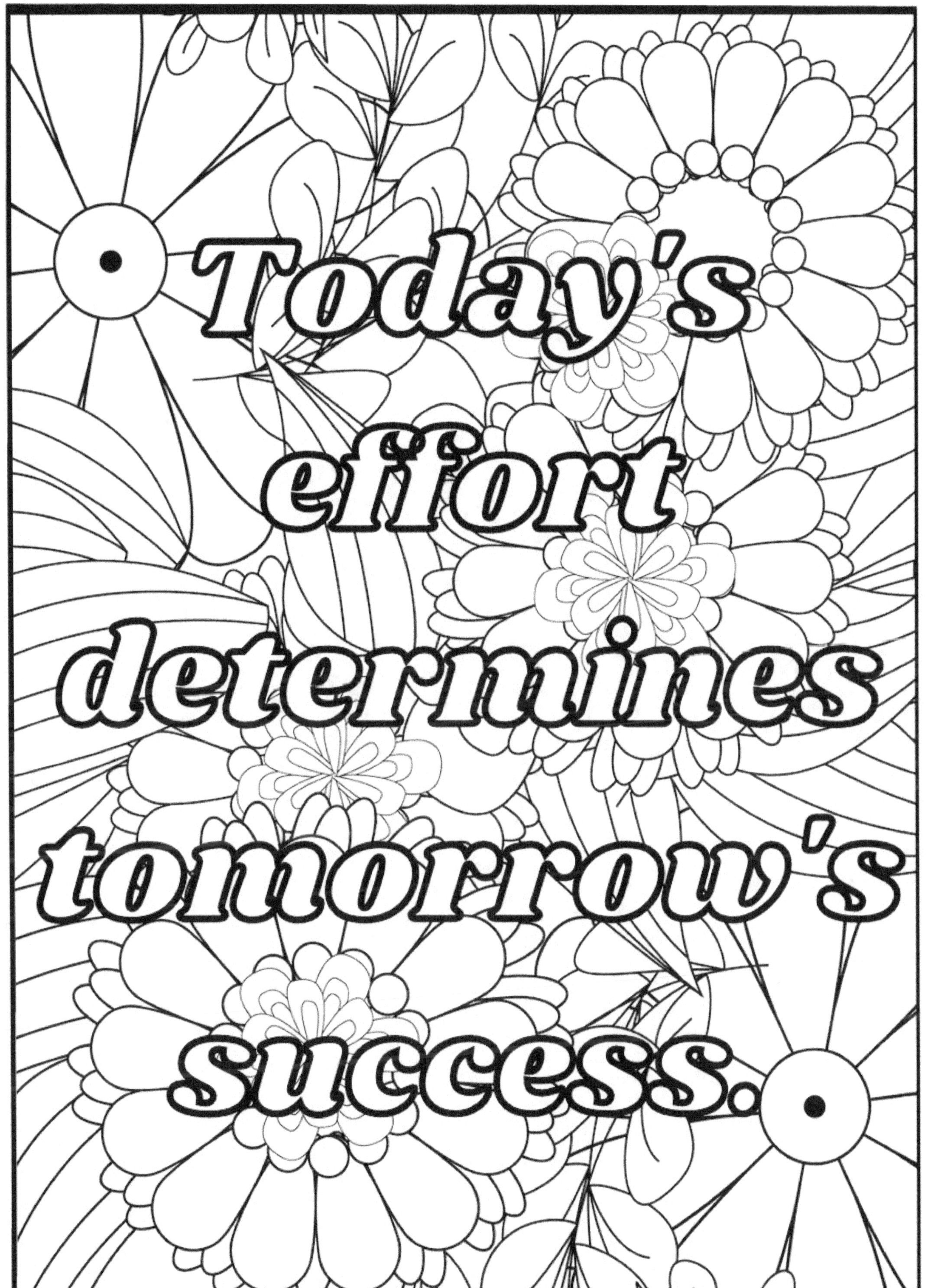

Today's
effort
determines
tomorrow's
success.

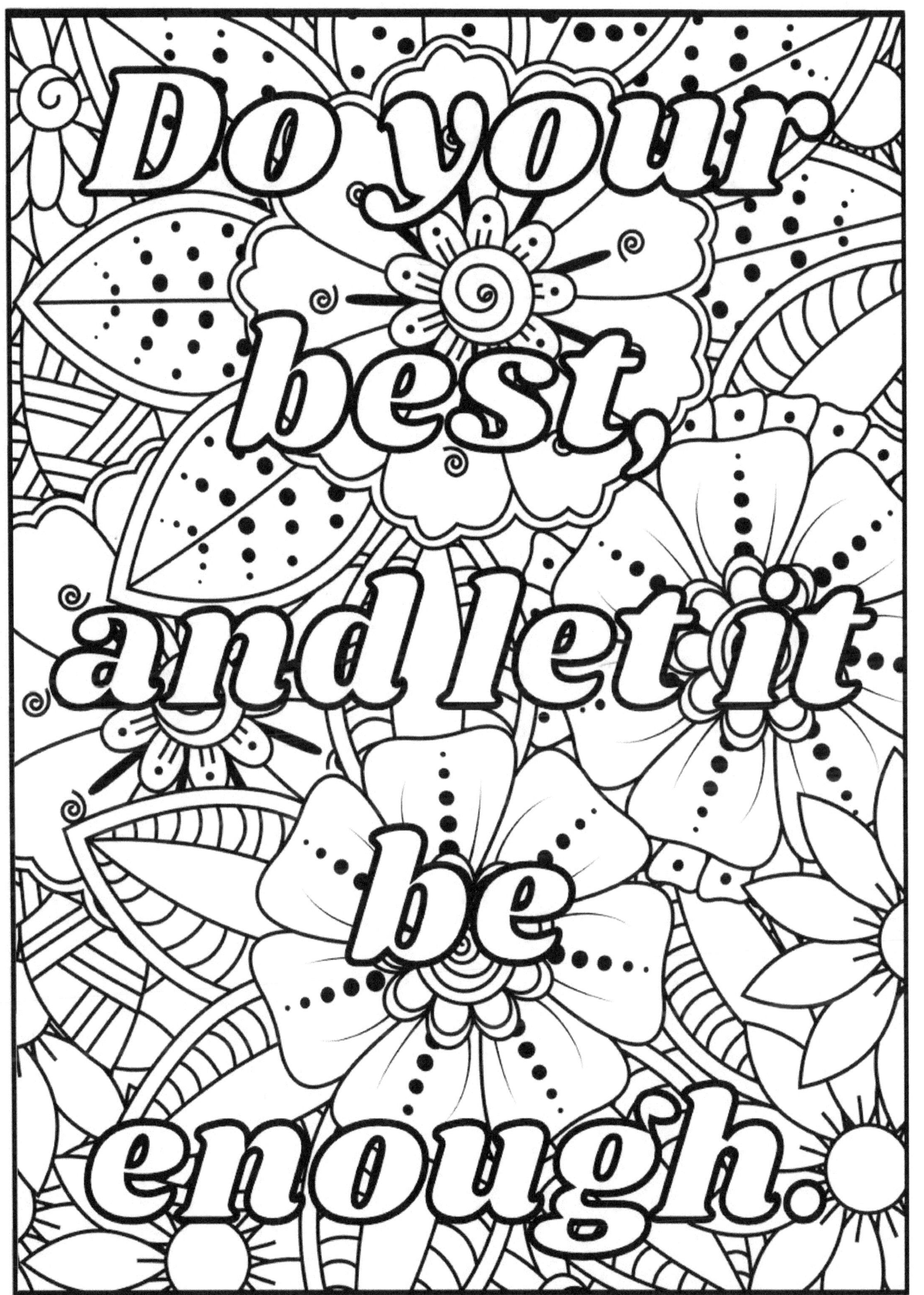

Do your best, and let it be enough.

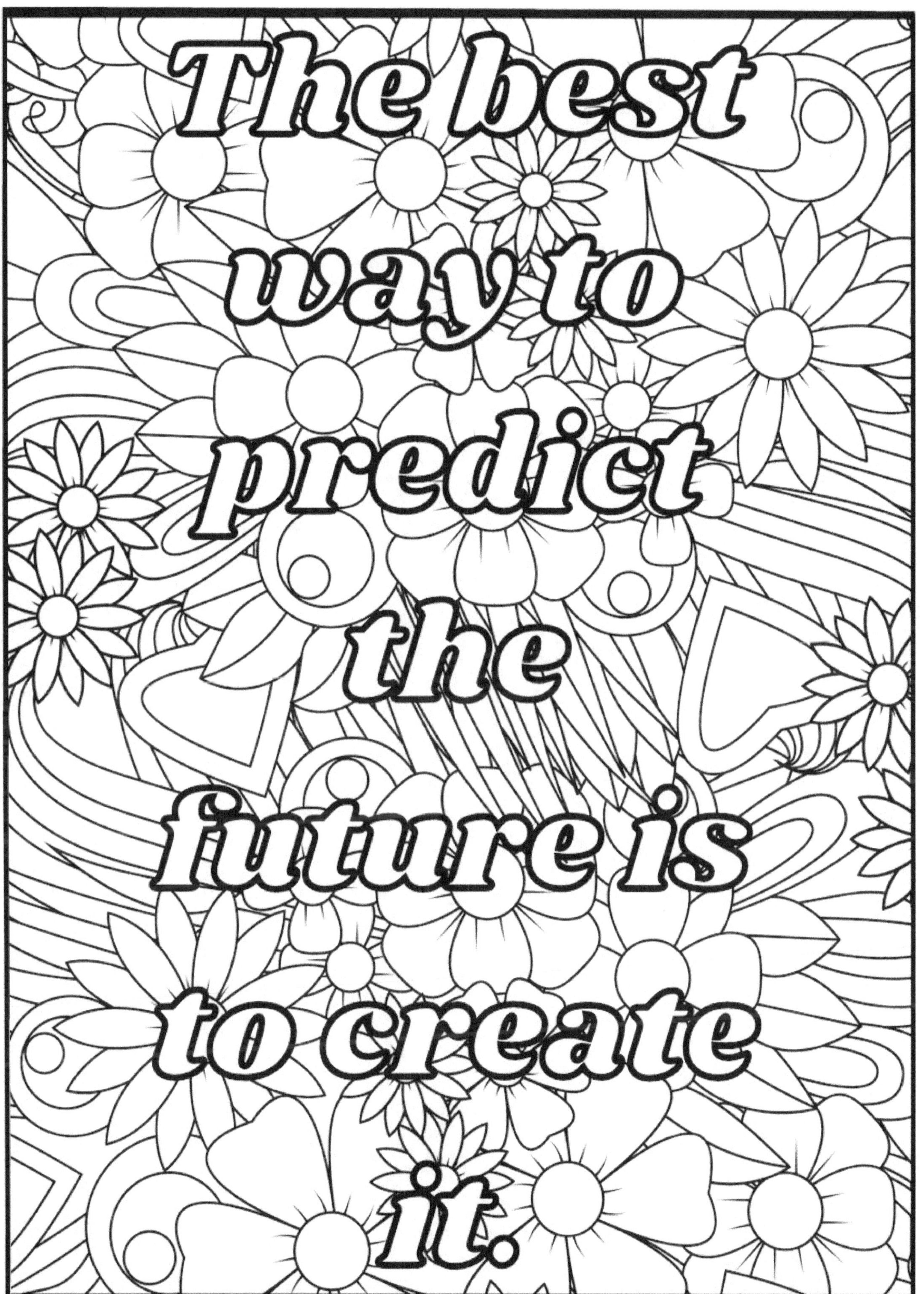

The best
way to
predict
the
future is
to create
it.

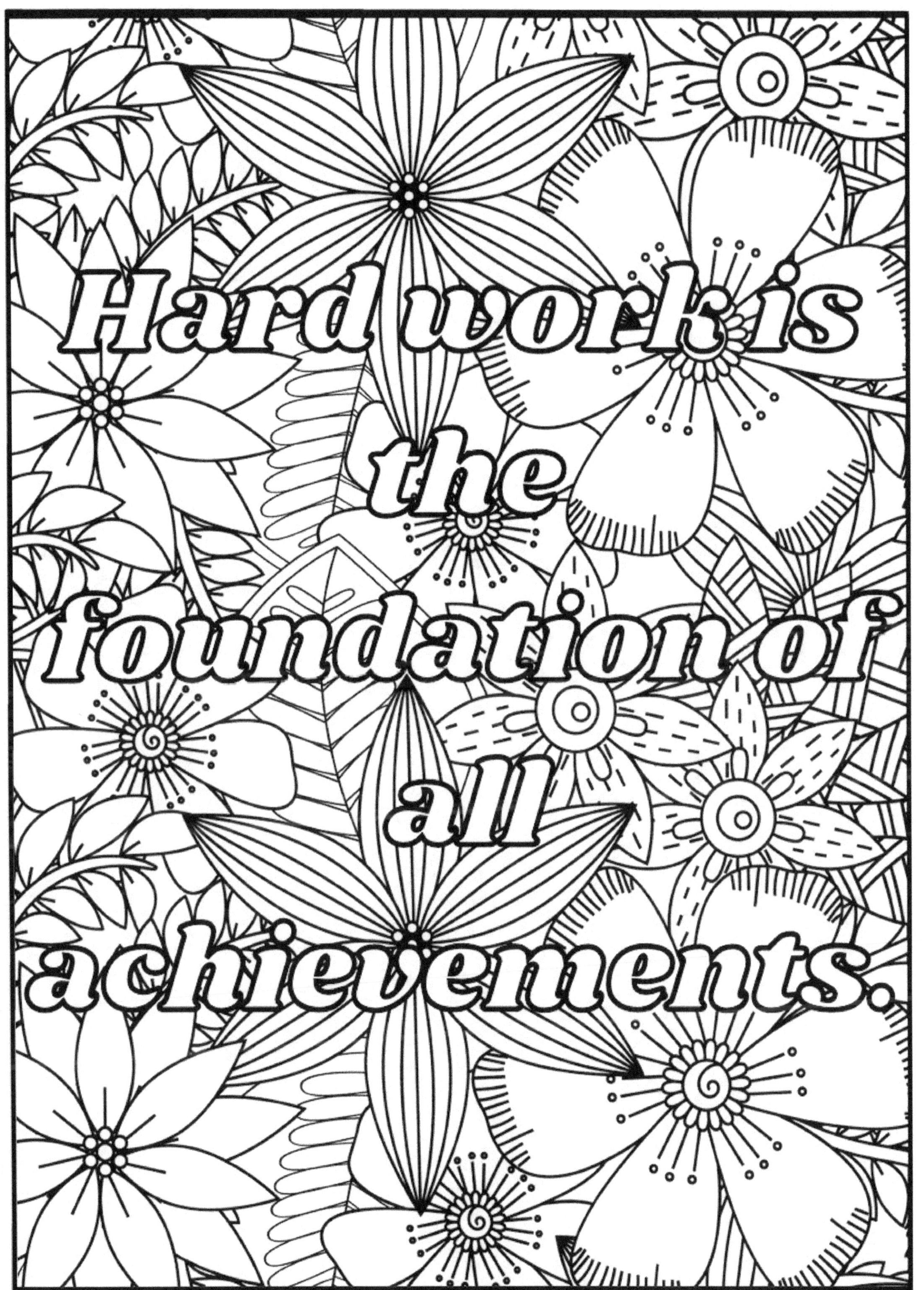

Hard work is the foundation of all achievements.

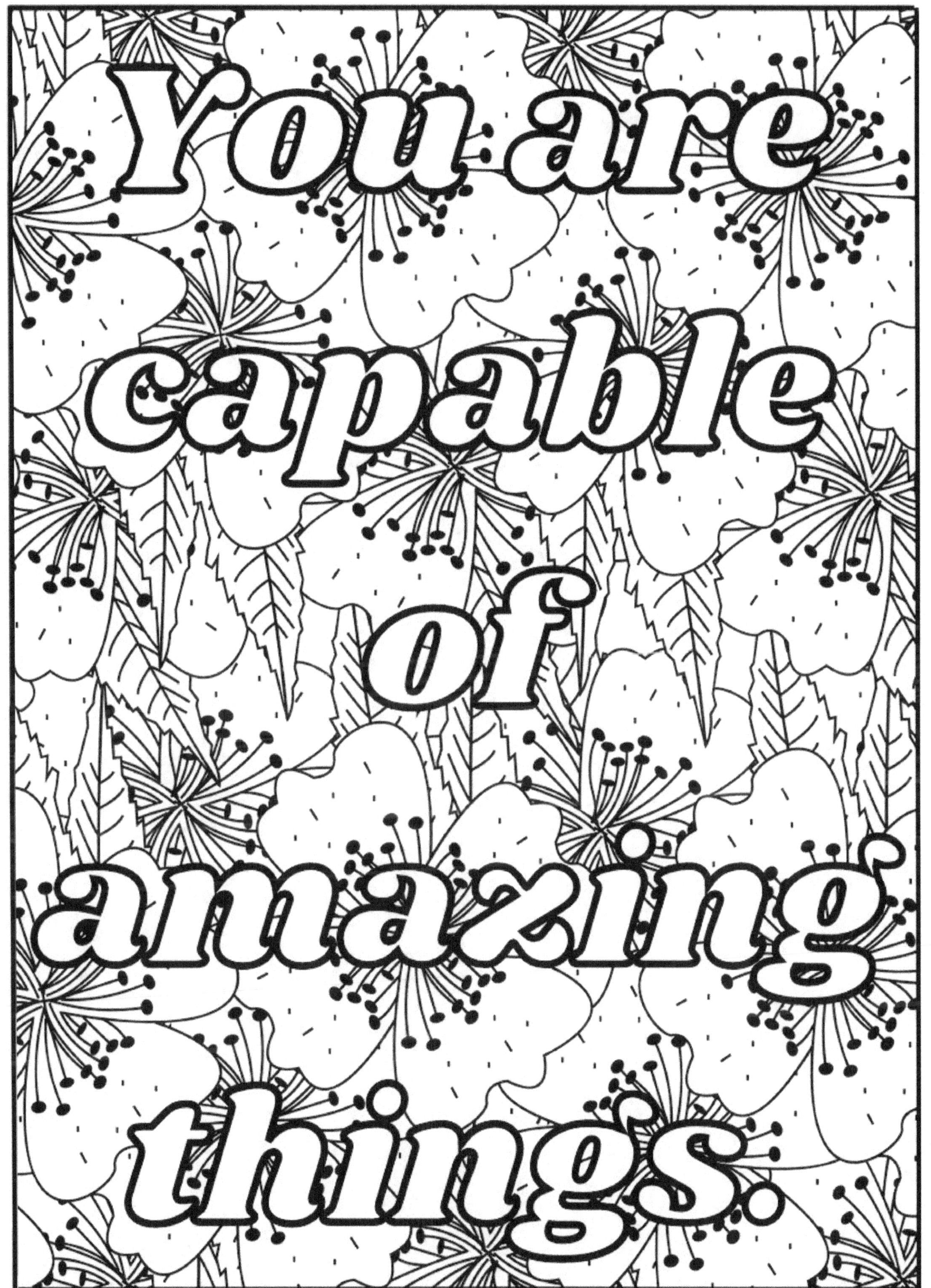

You are
capable
of
amazing
things.

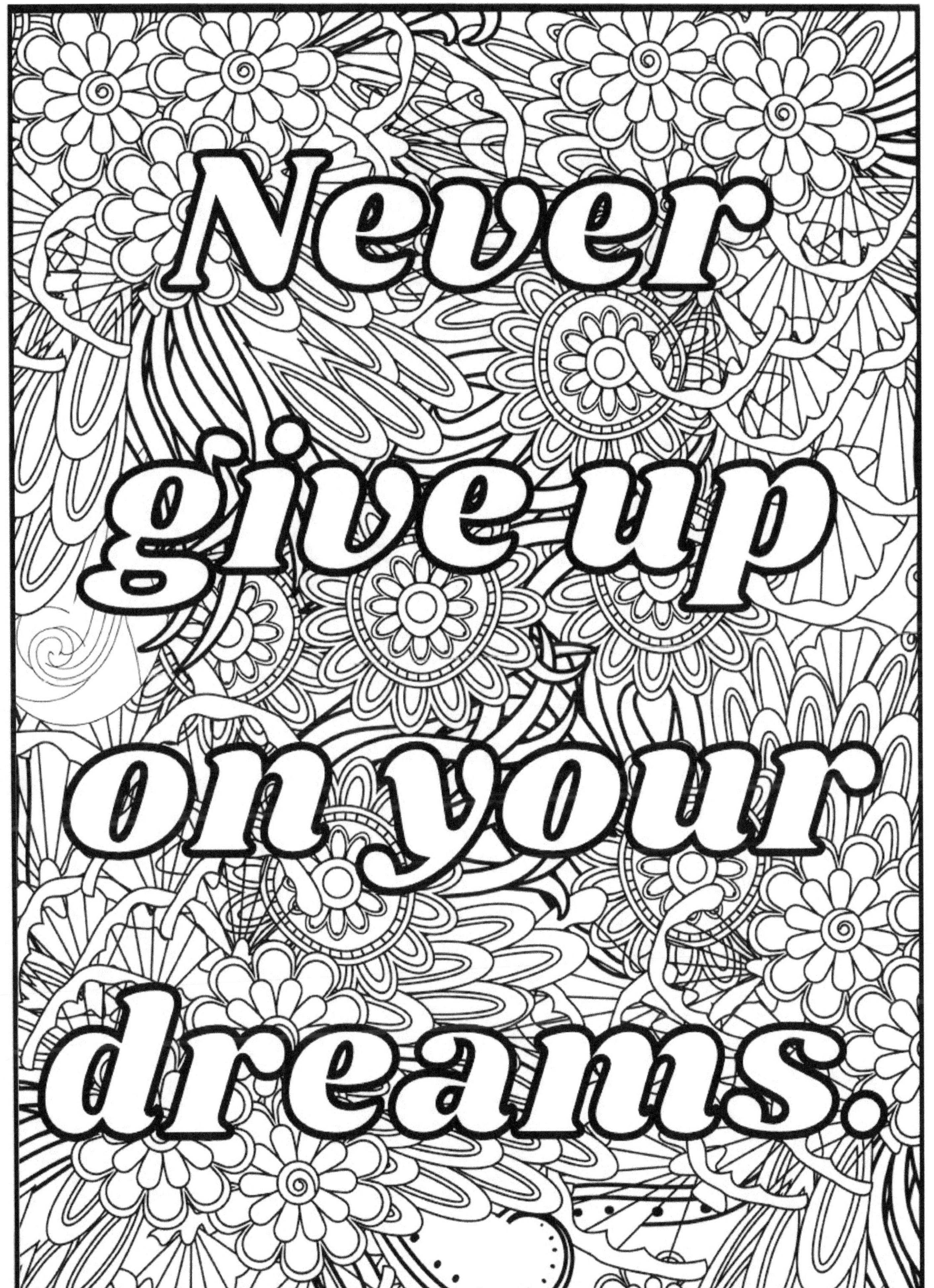
Never
give up
on your
dreams.

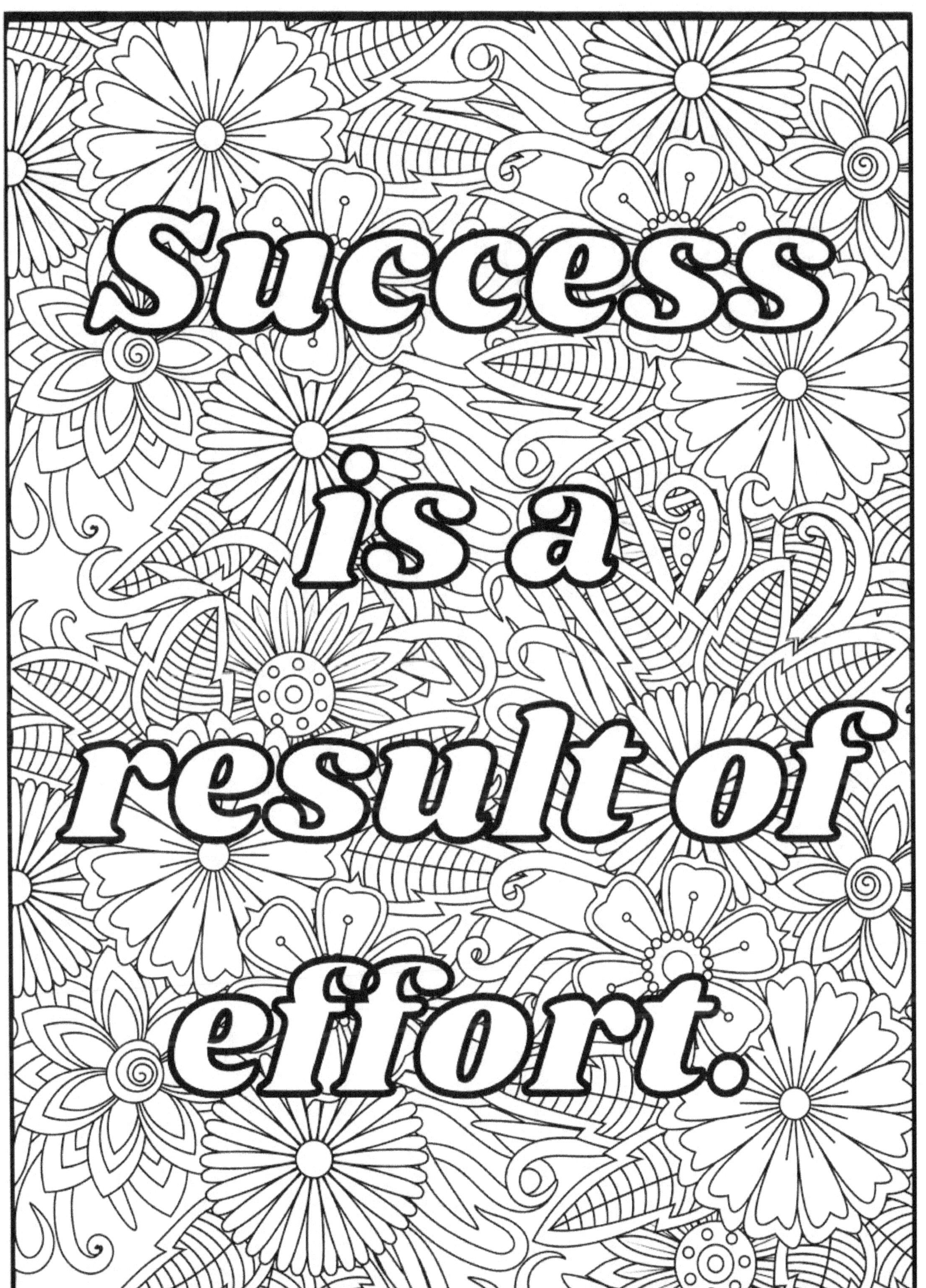

Success
is a
result of
effort.

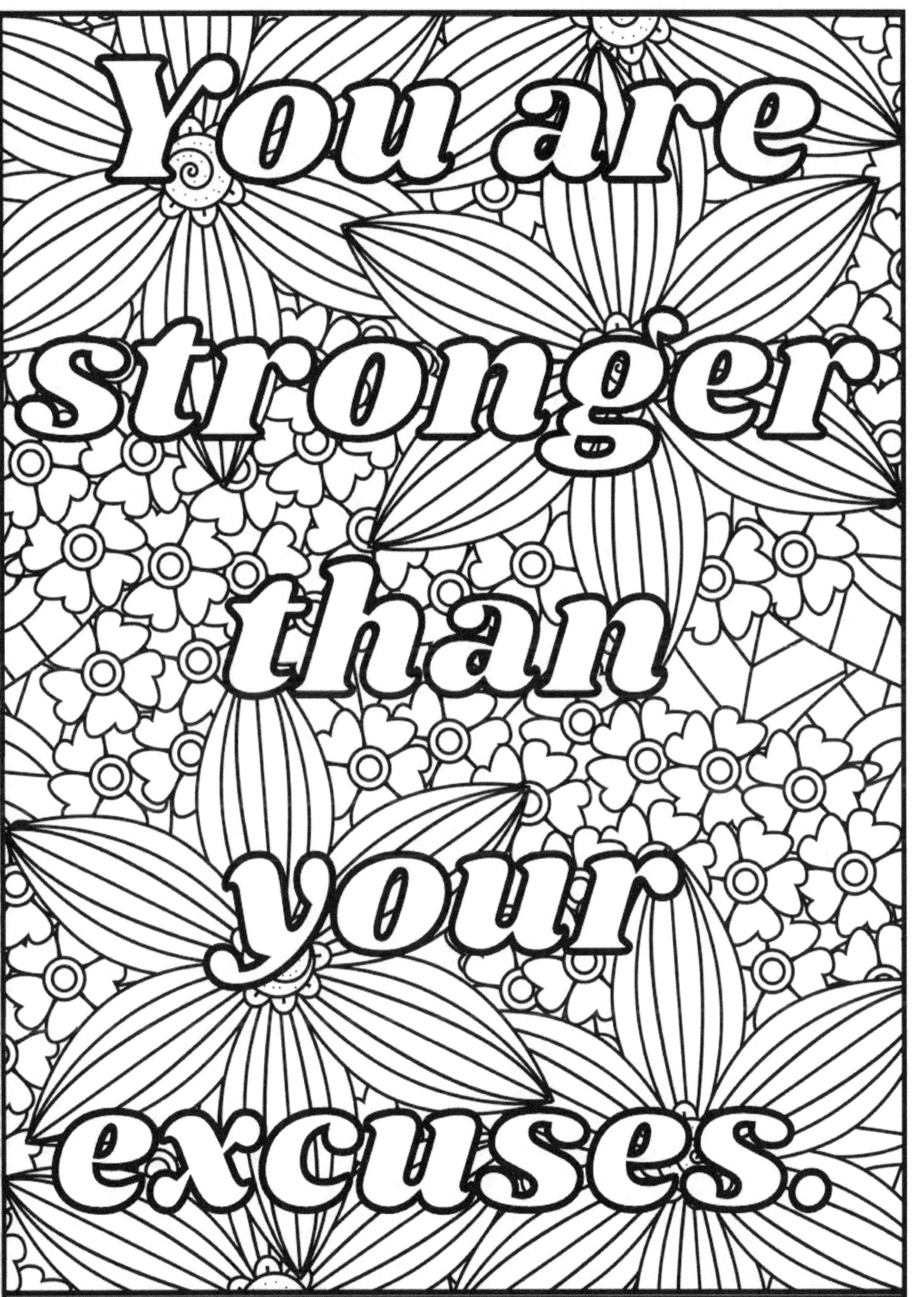

You are
stronger
than
your
excuses.

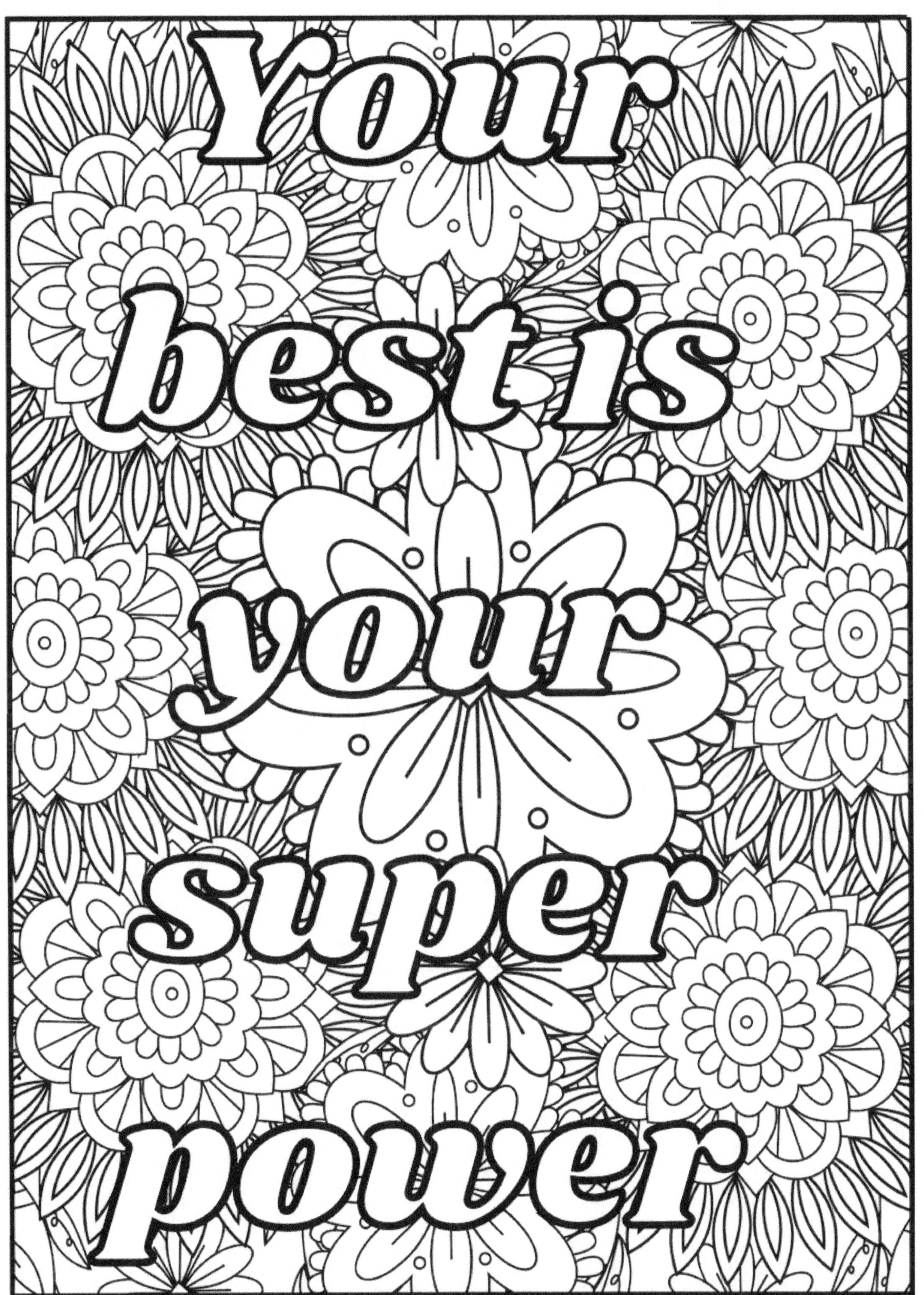

Your
best is
your
super
power

Enjoyed coloring this?

MORE BOOKS FROM THE AUTHOR

scan this with your camera